BORN WRONG, MADE RIGHT

Thinking Differently To Unleash Your Potential

Greg Stoughton

Praise for Born Wrong, Made Right

This book is a double thumbs-up! Having lived in a wheelchair for 50 years, I'm constantly on the lookout for stories of people who understand suffering, yet God-blessed victory through their trials. In Born Wrong, Made Right, Greg's practical, yet personal reflections will help you dig deep to realize your own potential through the grace and Spirit-sent provision given when we submit our hardships to our sovereign Lord.

Joni Eareckson Tada
Joni and Friends International Disability Center

If you're looking for a double shot of "real," you'll find it here. This is an inspirational reminder that none of us were born winners or losers—but choosers! Greg's story beckons us to courageously "faith" life's challenges, rather than run from them.

Doug Pollock
Author, *God Space: Where Spiritual
Conversations Happen Naturally*

Greg's drive might have been rooted in the exhortation of a special coach to climb "the pegboard" as a youth, but this fun, easy-to-read story leaves no doubt that his eventual embrace of God's grace through Christ helped him scale situations of challenge. You'll relate to, and learn from, many of the life lessons he openly shares and the thought-provoking questions he provides.

Rita McKenzie Fisher
Author, *Lessons from…* series (sports devotions)

I loved it when Greg helped coach youth camps during our years together at Athletes in Action. He always handled himself in such a way that you didn't realize he had any deformity. He has a great peace with who he is because of his faith in Jesus Christ.

Lorenzo Romar   .
Associate head coach, men's basketball, University of Arizona

iii

Working closely with Greg the past seven years, I have seen how extremely well he handles his physical differences with grace and ease. He has some good things to teach us all. Who among us hasn't wished that God made us without certain weaknesses? Greg's life story is a good reminder that God makes no mistakes, and a life of the fullest meaning and purpose is found through a personal relationship with Jesus Christ.

Steve Douglass
President, Cru/Campus Crusade for Christ

It's our business to help people realize their potential—wrong-thinking too often a part of their challenge. The perspective and inspiration of this book can help you (or maybe someone you know) to rise above limitations, break barriers, and live life more abundantly.

Matt Suter
Retired Procter & Gamble Manager; Advocare Distributor

Greg's life story personifies Psalm 139:13-14—that God knows each of us intimately, even in our mother's womb, where we are "fearfully and wonderfully made." In the physical sense, no person is born wrong. Greg's journey takes us from his birth defects to "wrong" happenings and "really wrong" choices. He shows us how great joy is found when we're "made right"—spiritually taken from "deformed" to "reformed." What an inspiration!

Kevin W. McCarthy
Author, *The On-Purpose Person: Making Your Life Make Sense*

Greg shares his story in a personal, vulnerable and transparent way. I loved it. I was encouraged, inspired and uplifted to read about this life journey that I could easily relate to, well beyond his physical deformities. I personally identified with many of the lessons he's learned, and I'm confident you, too, will greatly benefit.

Mark J. Goldstein
President, Central Florida Christian Chamber of Commerce

I loved the book! Born Wrong, Made Right is a compelling story of courage in the face of challenges; of grace in the midst of brokenness; of love conquering loneliness; of the secret to victorious living.

Dr. Harold B. Graves, Jr.
President, Nazarene Bible College

Leadership starts with authenticity. Greg's story captures us because of his willingness to bear his soul. Good questions help us to grow our hearts. Let the questions he asked himself, and those he offers us to consider, help fuel you toward realizing your God-given potential.

Lillie Nye Cashion
Executive Life Coach, Integrated Relationships

God desires to write a story in your life, that reflects His design of you. Greg's story is an example of this very thing and will provide you with an inspiring picture of how you can partner with God to see His imprint upon your life.

Don Cousins
Lead Pastor, Discovery Church, Orlando
Author, *Unexplainable: Pursuing a Life Only God Can Make Possible*

Every life holds a story waiting to be told to the world. Through Born Wrong, Made Right, Greg tells his story—the struggles, the setbacks along with the glimpses of hope and the settled redemption that faith and hope unleashes. May this work inspire you to live out your God-given potential.

Eric Swanson
Co-author, *The Externally Focused Church*

At the YMCA, we are passionate about finding wholeness in one's Spirit, Mind and Body. This book will help you find it!

David Newman
Sr. Pastor, Antioch Church (Lebanon, Ohio, YMCA)

You'll find Greg's story remarkable, fascinating and compelling on many levels. Well beyond his physical deformities, the life realities he's experienced are common to most of us. This book is a great and uplifting reminder that in God's eyes, every person is one of infinite value and worth, with an identity secure in Jesus.

Jack Alan Levine
Seven-time Author (*Live a Life That Matters for God*)
Speaker, Businessman and Addiction Expert

What joy for me to learn that more than three decades ago my life intersected with Greg's at such an important time in his spiritual journey. It's exciting to read about how he's grown, through all sorts of circumstances to experience a life abundant in Christ.

Jeff Wells
Senior Pastor, Woodsedge Community Church
Spring, Texas

When I enter our Athletes in Action World Headquarters each day, a vision wall reminds me of Greg's creative work and of his uniqueness, which in turn wonderfully reflects God's masterful creativity through us all. I'm grateful his story continues to help countless youth and others.

Mark Householder
President, Athletes in Action

The ease with which Greg carries himself and his courage to speak passionately from his heart has been of significant influence in my life. I'm always eager to clear my calendar and meet for a guaranteed inspirational visit when he's in town. Thanks for sharing your story, Greg.

Mike Prescott
Executive Leader (Banking Industry)

I'm so glad Greg has shared his story in such a personal, quality way. His life as one outwardly deformed is but a small part of his journey. Instead, God's inner work on his heart truly amazes and has allowed him to have such influence. Read his story, and you'll be blessed!

Mark Thurman
CEO, Dynatect

Greg's story illuminates one of the most difficult yet encouraging truths of the Christian life. God does not expect or want us to come to Him in a perfect form. He desires to work in and through us as we are—broken and imperfect—to accomplish His work. It can be a great challenge to wholly embrace this profound grace, but Born Wrong, Made Right makes it real, encouraging, inspiring and uplifting.

Bob Creson
President/CEO, Wycliffe Bible Translators, USA

Greg never saw his physical challenges as limitations, but approached life with a can-do attitude. His inspirational story will encourage you to keep going, no matter what obstacles you may face.

Stephanie Zonars
Assistant Athletic Director, Cedarville University

Greg tells an engaging story of his life that is both inspirational and instructive. His journey illustrates how we might come to handle an apparently overwhelming outward deficiency only to find that on the inside dwells a more significant malady of the soul that One stands ready to heal.

Ron Touby
Executive Leader, At Work On Purpose;
CruCity Director, Cincinnati

Born Wrong, Made Right
Thinking Differently to Unleash Your Potential

To Mom and Dad
You started it all.
Thanks for choosing to unconditionally love and
embrace what you were given.
I love you.

To Linda
Your love is astounding.
Thanks for your unconditional love
and acceptance of me.
I love you.

To Kyle and Ryan
To my terrific sons with whom I am well-pleased;
I love you.

To Friends, Colleagues and Teachers
There are way too many of you to name.
I am a better person because of you. Thank you.

To God, My Creator
You fashioned me fearfully and wonderfully in my mother's womb.
Through Jesus, You've changed my eternal destiny.
I love You.

CONTENTS

ACKNOWLEDGMENTS

I couldn't have written this book without the encouragement and contributions of many gifted friends, colleagues and professionals. To those mentioned, and likely to a few I've inadvertently missed, I'm grateful for the help I've received.

Special thanks to Nelson Gomez and a small band of brothers. Your praise of my initial blog, Nelson, and your frequent reminder to "Fulfill your purpose, Greg" launched this work.

Paul Konstanski: Thank you so much for sharing with me some of your time and giftedness. Your architecting of my story provided a sure foundation. Well done, my friend.

Jack Alan Levine: This project was dead a year ago. God used you to resuscitate it. Thank you for that and for your availability and guidance through this process.

Jim Moore: Your gracious offer to gift me timely, quality edits of huge need—not just one, but two—majorly advanced this project and deeply touched my heart. Thank you.

Jennifer Lechliter and Rita Fisher: Thank you both for the "heavy-lifting" (edits) you provided early-on.

Ron Touby: You did it again. Your wise insight and willingness to invest in my life and leadership have proved invaluable. This time, a conversation led to chapter-ending questions that added value to this work and its readers. Thank you.

Thank you to Karen Zando, Anne Marie Winz, Judith Neibling, Janice Kennedy, Les Stobbe, Dan Benson, Tom and Dena Yohe, Gail Porter, Tez Brooks and Bob Mac Leod for your inspiration, encouragement, critiques, edits, proofing and/or guidance.

Thanks to Mark Goldstein, Central Florida Christian Chamber President—a "champion" of this work. Thanks to friends and chamber members: Kevin McArthy (purpose coach), Jody Swaim (encourager extraordinaire) and to a host of you who gave of your time to read and offer input significant to this book's refinement.

Thank you to the following folks: Amanda Brown (final edits); David Welday (marketing consultant/coach with Higher Life Publishing); and Cheri Cowell, Kristen Veldhuis, Dawn Staymates and the publishing team of EA Books. You did it. You helped get this book across the finish line!

And I shudder to think who I'd be if not for colleagues with Cru who've contributed to my life and story. So many of you—fantastic bosses, trainers, mentors, life-coaches, and special friends—have powerfully and profoundly shaped me professionally and personally. Thank you.

I'm indebted to each of you who has generously partnered with us in our twenty-five years of service with Cru—grateful for your investment of prayers and giving. Thank you.

Thank you, Mom and Dad, for your unconditional love and acceptance of me.

And I'm incredibly grateful for my family. Thank you, Linda, for the amazing woman you are—for your acceptance of me, and for our twenty-five years of marriage. With enthusiasm, I look forward to our next twenty-five years—God willing. Thank you, Kyle and Ryan. My favorite title is that of "Dad." Thanks to each of you for your patience during this project. I love you all so much.

INTRODUCTION

The bell sounded, and students exited from the freshman English class I had just taught. As I turned toward my desk to prepare for my next class, an envelope met my gaze. On it, typed in all caps, was my name: MR. STOUGHTON

Curious, I picked it up and ripped it open to find a typed note. A part of it read as follows:

> DEAR MR. STOUGHTON,
>
> I REALLY DON'T KNOW HOW TO START THIS, SO I'LL COME RIGHT TO THE POINT. THE FIRST TIME I WALKED INTO YOUR CLASSROOM I NOTICED SOMETHING. AS A MATTER OF FACT I THINK THE WHOLE CLASS DID. YOU ARE PROBABLY WONDERING WHAT THIS NOTE IS ALL ABOUT, OR MAYBE YOU ALREADY KNOW. YES, MR. STOUGHTON, IT IS YOUR HANDS. ... INQUIRING MINDS WANT TO KNOW, SO MAYBE YOU SHOULD TAKE SOME TIME OUT OF YOUR BUSY SCHEDULE AND TELL US WHAT HAPPENED.
>
> SINCERELY, A CURIOUS KID

I glanced down at my hands. My first thought: *Why should I? I mean, it's such a small thing.* I'd known a few people with deformities who seemed genuinely handicapped. *That isn't me.*

My mind flashed to Mr. Faxon, a third-grade teacher and an inspiring role model. He maneuvered himself about the room using crutches, having been stricken with polio as a young adult. *Now that's a story! What would I share? What would I say?* "Inquiring minds WANT to know." *Really, are others that curious?*

Whether you like it or not, how you live affects others. And how you think about yourself affects how you live. In sharing with you some of my story, I hope you will find solace in knowing that your own imperfections (be they physical, emotional, circumstantial or mental) don't have to limit you—any more than what you ultimately achieve doesn't have to define you. Perhaps my journey will give you a fresh wind that pushes you further along in your own journey—a nudge in the right direction!

The student who wrote me that note reminded me that what others saw as a deformity, a disadvantage, I saw much differently. I didn't view myself as a person *born wrong.*

By the end of that school day, I decided I'd break from teaching the next day to tell my students what had happened. I'd talk to them about having been born with ectrodactyly, a rare genetic condition causing me to miss a few fingers and toes at birth, with some of those I have being fused.

By bedtime, I had decided I'd not just tell them about how I'd overcome this, and talk about my exploits, but I'd openly share about some of details of my first twenty-five years of life. They'd hear about my struggles as a teen, when circumstances beyond my control caused me to walk the hallways of the school they now attended (my alma mater) feeling downcast and depressed most days. They'd hear of poor choices I made in college as I tried to "do life my way" to satisfy my heart's desire to fit in and belong. They'd hear how sports, achievements and partying had failed to pacify an inner ache I felt.

They'd also hear the rest of the story. They'd hear about how I'd come to think differently and had begun to live differently, on a journey toward unleashing my full potential.

In words appropriate for the public school setting where I taught, they'd hear how at age twenty-two I had to hit bottom to realize my need for a personal relationship with Jesus Christ. They'd hear how through the words of the Bible—God's Word—I'd come to embrace myself as a person "fearfully and wonderfully made" by Him, my Creator.

I'd tell them how God was bringing positive changes to my life.

I didn't yet realize that although I'd been *made right* both physically and now spiritually (in Jesus), God wanted to help me *become more right* through a worthwhile, lifelong process of growth.

More than the student's reference to my hands, one phrase in the note bothered me. "SO MAYBE YOU SHOULD TAKE SOME TIME OUT OF YOUR BUSY SCHEDULE…" In an evening of personal reflection, I saw that in a desire to impress—to be the "perfect" teacher—I'd worked tirelessly. Yet I'd failed to be emotionally present (and real) with the students I was trying so hard to impact.

So the next day when I shared my story with each of my classes, I also apologized for my busyness and neglect—what I understood at that point about a more deeply ingrained flaw in my personal character. When I spoke to them, it was the first time I'd shared my story publicly—at least before so large a group. Later, I'd see how God used that day, and my need to pause and reflect on my life in preparation for what I would say, as a healthy step in my journey of personal and spiritual growth.

Over the months, years and decades to come, I'd see that I had lived a highly performance-based life. "Perfectionism" was a thread that had run through the fabric of my life. I'd learn how even as a boy (and well into my years as an adult), I had strived to compensate for my physical differences by trying to prove to others what I felt inside: that I wasn't a person who'd been *born wrong*. In my attempts to show that I mattered, I'd constructed an identity based on what I could achieve. I was in perpetual pursuit of the attention and accolades of others.

To My Readers

By now, you might think this is a book that looks to teach. It isn't. Simply put, this book tells the story—God's story—of my life.

Now, that said, I'm a former teacher and one who values personal growth. So whether you're a student, parent, person in the workplace, or in any stage of life, my story (and the stories I share) hopefully will stir you to give thought to your life. You'll snicker, draw inspiration, grimace at my miscues or, perhaps, be reminded of a hurt you've encountered. For us all, some pain is a part of our stories.

"Rethink It" questions at the end of each chapter provide you opportunity to reflect on your journey as a person of worth and incredible potential to God, our Creator. He is One who makes no mistakes or junk.

Born Wrong, Made Right will challenge you to think differently. It may help you to embrace some God-given reality of your life: a physical feature, personality quirk, or some circumstance well beyond your ability to control. Or you may become inspired to overcome some perceived limitation. It might motivate you to accomplish something you never thought possible. Or, if like me, you have achieved much and grown weary of how quickly the fulfillment of what we do fades, you may be ready to take a critically important, significant step of faith. God wants to change how you think. Who He is, and who you are in relationship to Him, matters more than anything you'll ever do. Get this, and you will move toward unleashing your full potential.

You might choose to read and discuss the questions at the end of each chapter as a family or in the context of a small group. This could help nudge you, or a person you know, toward some positive life change. *(Note: While parents of special needs children might find my story of interest, it is not written to this select group.)*

Wherever you find yourself in life—with or without a deformity— may my journey encourage you to make the most of yours.

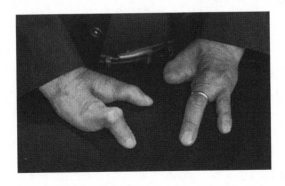

CHAPTER ONE

Beginnings

Children are likely to live up to what you believe of them.

Lady Bird Johnson
Former First Lady of the United States

I felt the thick arms of Richard "Coach" Newberry, my sixth-grade physical education teacher and basketball coach, envelop my waist. He hoisted my small, four-foot frame a couple of feet off the ground toward the bottom of a vertical, oblong board affixed to the wall. Two thick pegs, about ten inches apart, protruded from the bottom of two rows of holes that ran upward for about six feet on a climbing obstacle called "the pegboard."

"Hoss," middle linebacker of the eighth-grade football team and Coach's aide, had made a climb up and back down the board look easy. With freakish, Popeye-like forearms and a body that dangled yet hardly swayed, Hoss had completed the task in the time it took most of us sixth graders to do a single push-up. Only a few of my peers, mere mortals by comparison, had finished the task before my turn came.

I thrust my left arm skyward for the lowest peg and cupped the half-thumb and two fingers of my left hand around it. The higher peg to the right beckoned me to do likewise with my right thumb and its single, elongated finger.

Then Coach let go.

I dangled a nanosecond before losing my grip to fall on the mat.

Coach scooped me up.

Well, that's that. I tried. Now it's time to play basketball with the others.

Coach Newberry was a family friend. He'd heaped praise on me since the day we met, when we watched Super Bowl III together in his living room my second-grade year. In his early thirties with a sturdy frame, steely eyes, and a deep voice, he was a man's man who could project an intimidating front. But I had come to know his softer side. In his PE class, my favorite subject, the two of us had grown close.

That day, though, his softer side was nowhere present. My sweet thoughts of basketball rapidly soured when Coach said, "Greg, you have seven days to get up and down this board, or you won't pass this part of my class."

What happened to Coach? I didn't get how he could think someone with my pathetic grip and upper-body strength could ever climb this board of torture—a contraption suited for TV's Ninja Warriors before their time. Coach was exercising tough love, but his insistence that I peg myself up and back down the board stunk. Swept into woe-is-me mode, I did what little boys do. I ran home to Mom and whined.

Mom's usual kind and caring soul was gone too. "If Coach thinks you can do it, I imagine you'll find a way," she said. "Try your best and let's see what happens."

Days later, Coach Newberry's large hands again cupped my tiny waist. Lifted high, I instinctively thrust my left hand toward the peg.

"No," said Coach, causing me to halt. "Let's try it a different way. Can you throw your left arm over that peg?"

I did as he suggested and hooked the inside of my left elbow over the peg.

"Good!" he encouraged me. "Now swing over to the other peg and throw your right arm over it."

Looking a bit like a chimpanzee in a zoo, I alternated pegs on the insides of my elbows. I teetered back to the left, then right, and left again—back and forth—working my way up and down that board. Exhausted, I fell to the mat below. I did it!

My insides swelled with satisfaction as Coach lifted me to my feet. He wrapped me in his giant arms and gave me a congratulatory squeeze. "Super job, Greg. I'm proud of you."

He pointed to the stage with a twenty-foot vine strung from the ceiling. "You see that rope up there?" Find a way to make it up and down. You've got seven days." I was on to the next challenge.

Days later, I wrapped my few fingers around the thick twine and lifted my body a few inches off the ground. Quickly, I threw my legs tightly around the rope and then locked my ankles to maintain the progress I'd made. Repeating this, I inched my way up and then back down that rope. I climbed it once, twice, and then seven consecutive times—six more than required—before I dropped to the mat, fully spent.

By that time, at age twelve, I had grown to love opportunities to overachieve and impress others. I reveled in the rush of adrenaline with every accomplishment and the words of encouragement that followed ("Atta-boy; way to go, Greg!"). I compensated for my lack of fingers and toes by doing things in creative ways that worked. Often I dug deep to fight through physical or mental challenges with effort and grit. Triumph over obstacles helped me to feel confident and secure as a youth. I believed I could tackle whatever I faced. Life was like a tiger I swung by its tail.

A Beautiful Baby Boy

The encouragement I got from role models like Coach Newberry and Mr. Faxon was significant. However, my parents first instilled in me a positive, can-do attitude. To them I owe much.

In the fall of 1960, my mom, only a few months married, felt unusually nauseated. She emerged from a doctor's office having heard "the rabbit died." Five decades ago, there was no simple way to test for pregnancy. If a doctor thought a woman pregnant, she collected a urine sample and then injected it into a small animal (often a bunny). If she was pregnant, a hormone named human chorionic gonadotropin (hCG) would concentrate in the ovaries of the animal, causing them to mature. In order to determine this, the lab

4

had to cut the animal open. Pregnancy or not, the rabbit died. But in my mom's case, she was with child.

Seven months later, in June 1961, Dad took Mom's hand in hers, and they strolled across a parking lot and into the lobby of Portland's Good Samaritan Hospital. No sirens blared. They used no emergency entrance or wheelchair. Instead, up the elevator, down a long hallway, and into a room they walked. It was a drab and dreary room of gray walls and dim lights that brought my mom no joy.

The hospital room was but an exclamation point on a miserable nine months for Mom. She'd been horribly ill throughout the pregnancy—even though obstetricians at the time focused more on the health of the mother than that of the fetus. Ultrasounds weren't widely available until the late 1960s, so parents knew little of the child's gender, health or development. Because my mom was continually nauseated, her obstetrician prescribed a number of medications to try and help.

While nothing worked very well, she questioned little of what the doctor advised. People of that era generally accepted the judgment and practices of their medical professionals. They were the "experts." So when Mom's obstetrician diagnosed a supposed valve issue with her heart, she went to a specialist—the obstetrician's husband. He told her she would need surgery soon after she delivered. In the end, my mom had no surgery, but the thought of it added stress to her already difficult pregnancy.

By her arrival at the hospital, Mom had wearied of it all. Tired of even the stretch pants and tent-like smocks she wore to cover her protruding belly, she was ready to deliver—eager for a baby to cradle and smother in love. Dad, meanwhile, had grown increasingly enthused. A three-sport athlete and letterman in high school, Dad hoped for a boy, a little buddy with whom to someday share his affinity for sports.

Once in her hospital room, Mom was greeted by a battle-axe of a head nurse (Mom's description). She refused Mom's requests to get up and walk, as doctors today would encourage. About midnight, six hours after their arrival, the nurse added to Mom's agony by saying, "Mr. Stoughton, this isn't happening anytime soon. One of us around here might as well get some sleep. How about you go home and get a good night's rest in your own bed?" He did, leaving Mom for hours alone in what looked and felt like a prison cell.

For Mom, the time passed slowly. As her pain intensified, she phoned Dad, "Bob, come back here right now." He followed her command and returned immediately to the front lines.

I, on the other hand, stubbornly remained in the barracks of her womb. Finally, twenty-four hours after they had arrived at the hospital, Mom was wheeled to a surgical delivery room. About 5:30 p.m. on June 5, 1961, my mom gave an epic push, and I was born.

Hours later, Mom still groggy, they called Dad to her room from a holding-tank area for expectant fathers. The obstetrician flew past Dad in the hallway. "Congratulations, Mr. Stoughton. You have a beautiful baby boy."

Dad reached the door of the room, turned right and entered to see Mom clutching me. Tears—not of joy, he sensed—flowed down her cheeks. "What? What's wrong, Jan?" Dad asked. "I've heard we have a beautiful baby boy."

Mom struggled to talk, overcome by the thought: *Our baby has been born wrong.* "Look. His hands and feet—all of them are badly deformed." She pulled back the blanket for him to see.

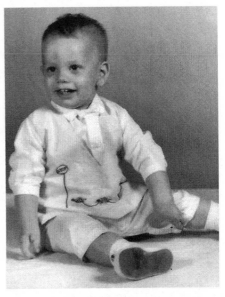

In disbelief, they stared at my tiny right hand, with a thumb and only one finger, elongated and bent inward at the second knuckle back from its tip. My little left hand consisted of a pinky fused to a long ring finger. What should have been an index finger was fused to my left thumb, and the middle finger was missing altogether—leaving a gap between the fused duos.

My feet had equally horrifying deformities, especially to new parents. My left foot had a big toe, a gap, and then two little toes to the left, webbed together. My right foot matched my hand with a big toe, a gap, and then a little toe that hooked back toward the center.

Expectations shattered, their spirits sank. Devastated, Mom pondered. *What happened? What went wrong? Could I have done something differently?* Drugged and exhausted, Mom drifted to sleep to deal with it all another day.

Distraught, Dad headed to the home of his folks—my Grandpa and Grandma Stoughton—who were also upset. Dad had gotten his hoped-for boy, yet he couldn't quiet his disturbing thoughts. *With hands and feet like these, he will never play sports. Why us? Why this? What will we do?*

A Significant Choice

News spread quickly of my defects and my parents' concern. Several people came to the hospital to visit. Grandpa and Grandma Stoughton were often present, and on occasion, Grandma Shroll, widowed, quiet and unassuming, slipped in to see me too. She'd comfort my mom with her prayers. Brought up in a home of faith, Mom was used to this.

The concept of faith was new to my dad. Raised agnostic, he'd only recently pledged a commitment to the Lord, borne somewhat out of necessity for permission to court my mom. Church was a part of their lives.

Leila from the congregation also visited. She sought to offer some reassurance, saying, "God is not surprised by this at all."

Dr. Schuler, however, spoke the words that changed my parents' hearts and perspective forever. An older physician my parents had never met, he popped into their room one morning.

"You have a baby boy, wonderfully made." He paused to let his words press past their forced smiles. "You now have a decision to make. You can take your boy home and hide him in a closet, shelter him from the world, and treat him as if he doesn't exist. Do that and your son will be a freak. Or you can love and accept him, treat him as if he's normal, and see how things work out."

Dr. Schuler talked of adults he'd seen who had lost their fingers or limbs in accidents. These people, he explained, struggled from being aware of what they lacked. He thought that wouldn't be true for me. I could adapt and learn to do things with my hands and feet in ways that seemed natural to me.

His counsel was sweet to my parents' ears—a new song played in their hearts. Their paradigms altered, they agreed not to hide me. They wouldn't dwell on what had happened or live a moment longer with regret. They would make the best of the circumstances through the choice to unconditionally love their boy. They accepted the hands they had been dealt (pun intended). No reactions from family, friends or outsiders would move them to feel or act self-consciously. They had no need to feel embarrassed or ashamed. They would heed this doctor's words of wisdom and timely advice.

Later that day, Mom and Dad walked from the hospital and climbed into the front seats of their VW Bug. In the small Volkswagen, Mom was my safety belt. Wrapped tightly and cuddled in her arms—snugly to her bosom—I rode home. My parents would never glance in life's rearview mirror because of me. There was no looking back.

Rethink It

1. Everyone has limitations, whether visible or unseen. Take time to reflect and write down what you perceive as any deformity or limitation you have (physical, mental, emotional, other). This could include things like anger, impatience, a critical attitude, etc.

2. As you consider your answers above, which of these limitations were self-imposed versus things you were born with or inherited through no fault of your own?

3. As you give thought to various stages of your life (child, teen, young adult, adult) are there people who have caused you to be more aware of what limits you?

4. Which people don't see–or don't seem affected by–your limitations?

5. Write down or share about a time when someone's affirmation helped you move past a limitation.

6. Is there a time when your actions or words helped someone else move past their limitation?

CHAPTER TWO

Off to the Races

My heroes are and were my parents.
I can't see having anyone else as heroes.

Michael Jordan
National Basketball Association Great

First grade and Meet-the-Teacher Day invoked fireworks neither I nor my mom had anticipated. Mrs. Kenneth, my assigned teacher, told my mom that the principal, Mr. Brown, felt I should sit in a special-needs classroom because of my deformities.

Mom vehemently disagreed. After all, I had excelled academically and socially in kindergarten. Sure, I had been scared silly the day Mom grabbed my hand and walked me up the stairs into the home where Mrs. Hargett, my first teacher ever, taught her kindergarten class. By noon that first day, I'd made fifteen new friends and found a "cave" in her basement in which to have fun and explore.

With me in tow, Mom raced down the main hallway of Mary Harrison Elementary School and into the office door marked "Principal". Mom let him know with firm but courteous words that when school started, I would take a seat in Mrs. Kenneth's first-grade classroom.

At the end of the first day, Mrs. Kenneth called my mom. "Greg will do just fine. When the other kids asked him about his hands, he just smiled and said, 'It's okay. It's the way God made me.'"

Within days, Mr. Brown and I had bonded and become friends. Most afternoons I walked to his office so the two deformed fingers of my right hand could snatch pieces of candy from a large jar on top of his desk. I had no trouble latching on to treats.

My Earliest Years

In all of my preschool years, Mom and Dad followed the trail that Leila and Dr. Schuler had blazed. Surely, some people thought I'd been *born wrong*, but my parents rarely gave thought to my deformity.

Growing up, Mom attended to my needs and smothered me with affection. Even as a newborn, she took me out with her wherever she went. In hot summertime, she dressed me in shorts and short-sleeved outfits that left my hands and feet exposed. Mom wasn't showing off; she just didn't care what onlookers thought. Some people stared. Others asked what had happened. Mom would smile and reply, "He's absolutely fine. It's the way God made him. He loves him, and we do, too." Her words gave shape to what I said in first grade.

Coaxed by my parents' affirmation, I scooted around the house in a wheeled walker at just a few months of age. That got boring, so I found a way to wrap my legs around the walker's legs and dangle my torso over its edge. Hanging upside down, I taught myself to grasp objects with the opposable thumb and finger of my right hand.

By nine months of age, my balance was good enough to attempt my first step. Wearing standard infant shoes, I was off to the races. Walking, then running, led to scrapes and bruises—Mom a constant source of comfort.

She offered a shoulder to cry on or supplied a hug, kiss or Band-Aid® whenever or wherever needed. As I aged, Mom most often broke from her housework to help me work puzzles, play board games, color and more. My hyperactivity demanded her attention.

Well before that scary first day of kindergarten, Mom taught me to grip a thickly rounded, fat pencil and drag it across large-lined, grainy pieces of paper—how my generation learned to write. With love and much patience, she instructed me in making letters. Then with similar kindness and diligence, she helped me learn to read, setting me up to achieve. She made certain that by age six, I'd be ready for public school—even if it wasn't ready for me.

Prior to my start of first grade, our family twice moved to smaller communities in Oregon. First we moved from Portland to Roseburg (thirty-thousand people) and then to Toledo, a city of three thousand.

In Portland, my dad had worked as a certified Professional Golf Association (PGA) teaching pro. Although he loved golf, by my first birthday he'd wearied of the long and irregular hours he worked. He decided to change careers. In Roseburg, he landed a Monday-to-

Friday office job with the state's employment division, an agency he worked with for the next thirty years.

As Mom mostly nurtured, Dad was my teacher, trainer and coach. In Roseburg, Dad introduced me to chores. He set aside his golf clubs to instead swing a shovel, hoe and rake, landscaping the hill in front of our place. We were a team: Dad pushed the wheelbarrow; I rode in it. I slowed his progress; he never seemed to care. In my earliest years, Dad modeled for me what it meant to keep busy, be it landscaping, tinkering in the shop, or rarely missing a day of work.

Dad did all he could to help me become his sports buddy, and it worked. By age three, I had embraced his near-fanatical love of athletics. Almost before I could run, I knew how to throw, pass, shoot, dribble, kick, catch and swing a bat or a plastic golf club.

As a little tyke, I took snaps of the football from him. My plastic helmet strapped on, I would get the ball and tuck it tightly like we'd watched it done on TV. I'd pretend to snake my way through a few defenders, sprint the length of the yard, and cross an imaginary goal line to score a touchdown to Dad's cheers.

Dad demonstrated everything for me. Then he'd step back and let me clutch the object however felt most natural to me. I threw, shot and bounced a ball with my left hand. However, with a bat or golf club in my hands, I liked to swing right-handed. I've always had more strength in the grip of my left hand, allowing me to pull with my left side more rapidly through the hitting zone.

Dad also taught me life skills. I recall lessons on how to properly eat and how to tie my shoes. For a time, Dad let me shovel my food in left-handed, putting a stranglehold on the fork. "Son, that doesn't look good," Dad said. So I switched the fork to my right hand to shovel it in from the other side of the plate. Eventually, Dad got me to rest the fork atop the elongated finger on my right hand and pinch it with my opposable thumb to lift the food from my plate. It looked civil enough for a date with a girl, just not at age five.

Then one morning, Dad met at the front door to tie my shoelaces as he'd done each day before. "It's your turn today," he said. "You can do this." It was a tedious, trial-and-error effort too complicated to explain, but in a day or two I could tie my shoes on my own.

Surgeries and Showing Off

My preschool days of sports and play were temporarily interrupted when a pediatrician recommended I have surgery on my left hand. He felt that a surgery to separate the two sets of fingers fused on my left hand could improve my dexterity. Immediately after the procedure, he wrapped my left hand tightly. For a full week, I lay on a sofa in an aunt's home with my arm upraised, per doctor's orders. When the doctor returned from a hunting trip and opened the wrap, my little finger and the finger closest to it had separated perfectly. However, my thumb and the finger next to it had lost the blood needed to remain alive—gravity! The doctor had no choice except to amputate my finger and the upper portion of what is now my half-thumb. My parents were upset, but I adapted quickly. My hands have been this way ever since.

I've never felt pain in my hands, except for one spot on my left half-thumb where all the nerves from the amputation meet. Other than times I've banged that spot or have been poked there while wrestling with my two boys (having to cry "uncle"), the surgeries have been of more help than concern.

I also had two surgeries on my feet, but not until ages seven and eight. A podiatrist thought my balance (already good) might be better if an experimental procedure to try and straighten some of the curvature of my toes might help. Two consecutive summers, one foot at a time, the doctor replaced some tendons in my toes with inch-long pins that he  inserted and later removed. These surgeries didn't work. Within a few years, all my toes had curved back to their original position.

With one foot at a time immobilized, I had the opportunity to show off. While in a wheelchair, I learned to "pop wheelies." On crutches, I learned to take huge strides and beat my friends in short sprints. Nothing delighted me more than to prove to others I hadn't been *born wrong*.

Those years growing up, I never felt sad or sorry for myself. My sister Tami, born in Roseburg about the time I was three, felt it on my behalf. "I wish it were me and not Greg who had fewer fingers," Tami once told our mom. It was sweet of her to think that way, but having ten fingers might have messed me up. Things have worked out fine for me—just as I am.

My sister almost wasn't to be. Mom and Dad consulted several doctors as to whether to have a second child. *Would he or she arrive similarly deformed?* An obstetrician placed the odds of it happening at one in a million and convinced Mom that the medications she took while pregnant caused my problem. (Some genetic specialists in my twenties told me otherwise, but he may have been right.) While pregnant with Tami, my mom took nothing—not even aspirin. Tami, my lone sibling, was born free of birth defects.

Hello, Toledo!

Within a month of my sister's birth, we moved from Roseburg to Toledo.

During my parents' courtship, they'd pledged to talk with one another about everything—never to keep secrets. Apparently, my dad

forgot his promise. One night he burst through the door to say, "Honey, I took the job. We're moving." The two of them had taken a short trip to Toledo to check it out, but Mom hadn't yet agreed to make the move. My dad's

My sister, Tami, and me

announcement was a shock. "Would you like to commute, Bob?" Mom had asked my dad on a trip to scout the area. Perhaps he thought she was joking. She wasn't.

Toledo sits seven miles inland from Newport, which is a beautiful tourist spot on the central Oregon coast. However, there is nothing scenic about Toledo. Train tracks still run through its city streets, and its downtown shops are worn and weathered. The town's two stoplights and few local stores and family restaurants offer little in the way of excitement, especially for a stay-at-home mom.

Nevertheless, we left Roseburg and settled into a small duplex on a hill with a giant smokestack in plain view from the driveway outside. Aside from a few close friendships that evolved over time, the move never much suited my mom.

By first grade, and my episode with the principal, my opinion of Toledo was much loftier than Mom's. We'd moved across town from our original duplex into a brand-new home in a newly developed neighborhood. Our house backed up to a forest with a deep ravine. Nearby were miles of woods with bicycle trails nicely worn to explore with friends. There were train tracks to walk, an inlet to fish and open lots on which to play sports. Looking back, I couldn't have asked for a better place to enjoy a boyhood full of fun.

Rethink It

1. What things about you physically would you most like to change?

2. For these things, would it be better to address them with surgery? With changes in habits? With changes in the way you think about them?

    We shouldn't allow society's standards to tear us down or cause us to feel less beautiful. Peers, school activities like sports or drama, or certain careers (e.g., modeling), can pressure us to change our body image to meet the expectations of others.

3. Are there ways that you are allowing others to adversely affect what you think about your body?

4. List things about how you inwardly think, feel, believe or behave that you wish were different.

5. As you give thought to the internal things on your list, what might you do to change or minimize the limitation?

6. Are there things you say or do to validate your worth because of how you feel about your inner or outer self?

CHAPTER THREE

Boyhood Fun

The blessedness of being little!
William Shakespeare

Like most boys, I could have died any number of times growing up.

I came close one summer when Oregon blackberries were in season. I frolicked through briar patches and got scratched. I ate truckloads of berries for days—plain, as well as in Mom's homemade jam and pies. One afternoon, at age seven and unable to sleep at naptime, I begged my mom for water to quench my thirst. She eventually caved and entered my room to see me nearly swallowing my tongue. She phoned Dad, and together we sped to the doctor's office. Twenty minutes more and I would have died from an overdose of berries—simply too much of a good thing.

On another occasion, I shinnied up a tree with a friend climbing right behind me. I felt what I thought was the sting of bees. "You'd better get down now," I yelled, "or I'm coming down on top of you." On our walk home, I noticed a red circle on my wrist the size of a half-dollar coin. Mom phoned the utility company. We later learned the tree's limbs were touching a power line. Had it been a wet day, or even damp from that morning's dew, we would have fried from the voltage that surged through the line.

Mostly, I just took risks like kids do, giving little thought to what could happen.

I never cut off one of my few fingers, but I witnessed others' flesh wounds when we peeled the bark off chittum trees with our pocketknives. We skinned those trees bare as high as we could reach, leaving but a small strip of bark on each trunk to promote its future growth. Once the bark dried in the sun, we bagged and hauled it to the local feed store. The store then sold it to pharmaceutical companies, which used it to make laxatives. It was a great win-win. I put spending money in my pocket and helped keep America regular.

Some summer days, if I beat Mom down with my restlessness, she would toss me a dime and let me walk a mile from our home to a small local store. On a narrow and winding two-lane road, fully loaded log trucks sometimes breezed by. My ten-year-old legs would need to scramble up the roadside hill or into a gutter on the other side so as not to become road kill. Once at the store, I'd plunk my change on the counter and then wrap my fingers tightly around an ice-cold bottle of Coca-Cola®, quenching my thirst. I had tons of freedom to explore my world during those years.

My parents were permissive, yet safe. Dad never cut me loose on the power table saw, but aside from that, I didn't find much to be off-limits. As I tell my two boys now, the world was a safer place then.

Youth Sports and Sixth Grade

Constantly on the go, and in an era when video games consisted of "Pong," I played baseball, football and basketball as a youth. Dad's experience and gifted teaching, coupled with my drive to practice, made me well-versed in the fundamentals. Because of this, I was ahead of most kids my age when I first took the field or stepped onto the court. I knew what to do even if I couldn't quite do it right. I looked to improve, if not perfect, certain skills.

On the little league baseball diamond, I started at shortstop. I scooped up grounders and on occasion opened my eyes to find a fly ball tucked into the web of my glove. A lefty, I moved to first base. I got bored, and since my dad was team manager, I bugged him until he let me pitch. I took the mound and threw the only pitch I had: a "two-finger" splitter, slow and accurate, the ball floating precisely waist-high across the center of the plate each time. I gave up a dozen runs as the other team batted through its entire lineup. Dad trotted from the dugout and yanked me from the mound. Knowing I'd failed, tears trickled down my cheeks as I shuffled my way back to first base and never pitched again.

In basketball, I bounced the ball with my palm more than my fingertips, yet I found it easy to maintain a steady, controlled dribble. I first shot the ball with two hands, heaving it toward the rim. As I grew and gained strength, I could rest the ball on the palm of my left hand and place the two fingers of my right hand to its side to hold it steady. I'd bend my knees and push it up, learning to do so with soft rotation and a nice follow-through. Even in my preschool years I had pure technique—pure enough to once catch the basketball off the tap of a jump ball and swish a shot from twelve feet away… into the other team's basket. Fortunately, I made enough shots in the right hoop to also make a couple all-star squads.

I started playing football in fifth grade. Though small, 4'8" and eighty pounds, I loved to hit and tackle. But I didn't get to do it much. By sixth grade, I was primarily a specialist. For some reason, the little kid with just a few fingers was the only one out of forty who could bend at the waist, look back between his legs, and hike the ball with velocity and accuracy to the punter and holder on kicking plays. Because of my size, Coach Parks and I had an understanding. "Stoughton, snap the ball, drop to the ground and get out of the way," he said. "Don't even try to block. I don't need anyone killed on my watch." One game, I almost got killed. With our team up 16-0 in the final quarter, Coach Parks ran me in to take a few snaps as third-string quarterback. I got the play from the sideline to hand the ball to a running back. But I thought I'd display the strength of my throwing arm. The ball slipped from my hand, causing me to toss a short, high and wobbly pass into the hands of an opposing lineman. When I got back to the sideline, Coach Parks wanted to kill me.

I had an insatiable desire to compete, and an intense drive to excel. Even now, nearly fifty years removed, I have vivid memories of a few great practices—and the praise of coaches—or an instance when I shined on a play. One basketball game, I made a twelve-footer from the baseline and got fouled on the shot as time on the clock expired. We'd trailed by two points, so if I made the shot, we'd win! I did. A photographer captured my shot. The next week his photo appeared in the weekly county newspaper. A hero, I was the talk of the town, especially among the adults. It (and I) felt "cool." But just as fresh in my mind are the times, like on the mound, that I fell short of a coach's expectations—or, worse yet, my own. Either way, sports were dopamine for me then. Beyond the competition and fun, athletics gave me a venue to prove I was normal and were a source of my feelings of significance, value and worth.

During those years, I got teased some. But my esteem was pretty healthy, and I deflected most of the taunts I received. Mainly, just a couple of guys would pick at me to try and get under my skin. I'd hear phrases like "nice pinchers," or they'd try to imitate how my right hand looked by opening and closing the tips of two of their fingers. They sometimes did this while humming the theme song to the newly released movie *Jaws*.

One day, John, the class bully, thought he would take a break from smoking in the boys' room to beat me up. John wanted to meet me in the parking lot after school. Playing basketball, I'd made a close friend, Steve. Nicknamed "Stretch," Steve towered above the rest of us—six feet tall in the sixth grade. If a bit naïve, I wasn't a fool. I invited Steve to come with me for the fight. Steve walked up to John and said, "You touch him, and I mess up your face!" That put an end to John's bullying of me. After that, I never got teased much in junior high or all my years growing up.

Family Time

By sixth grade, my family seemed close.

For a couple of years, my folks had a hankering to camp. One June we first tossed our sleeping bags on a tarp at a campground near the base of Mount Hood in Oregon. One morning, we awoke like popsicles when the overnight temperature had dropped into the teens.

25

Another time we scurried to pack our tent to avoid a flash flood on a river in Eastern Oregon. Then, one week in Southern Oregon, we baked in 105-degree heat. And don't ask me why we once camped fifteen minutes from our home. During the night, the skies poured down rain. We practiced togetherness that night as we slept in our car, with our bedrooms (and beds) only a short drive away. Sometimes it felt like forced fun, but later we laughed over memories we shared outdoors.

In our home we'd sometimes gather around the table to play games. Often we simply enjoyed our pets (a dog, a cat, and a bird). Some evenings we'd watch shows like *Happy Days* and *M*A*S*H* on our living room TV.

One night my mom called my sister and me to the living room for a different activity. Mom had talked to Dad, thinking that as a family we should read the Bible and pray. My body was plopped on the piano bench, where Mom kept reminding me to quit squirming. Spiritual devotions—new and uncomfortable to me—seemed even more painfully awkward to my dad. Be it his changing priorities, busyness, or a conscious choice, the embers of the faith he had once professed had long ago been snuffed. Unless we traveled an hour to Sheridan, Oregon, to visit my mom's sister and her husband—my Aunt Jean and Uncle Mike—and attend services where my uncle pastored, we rarely went to church.

About the time we experimented with devotions, Mom insisted that Dad give Sunday worship another try, as they had done back when they dated. Once at church, I realized that if listening to my dad fumble through ten minutes of reading Scripture and prayer was difficult, my butt on a church pew hearing some other guy drone on for an hour was even worse. Within weeks, Dad didn't much want to go and Mom grew weary of prodding him to attend. That ended our spiritual training. Personally, I felt relieved.

Christmas Eve of 1972, at eleven years old, I looked forward to Christmas Day. It was a white Christmas that year, and a massive snowfall had slowed the anticipated arrival of an uncle from California. Glad to give him my bed when he arrived, I tossed a sleeping bag on the floor at the threshold of my bedroom. It was the perfect spot from which to watch Santa Claus work. I saw him with my own eyes. My dad slipped past me down our hallway carrying a bright yellow, Schroeder-like piano in his arms. That was atop my sister's wish list. I watched for a hockey game to pass by. It didn't, but I had no doubt that in the morning I would find it beneath our tree.

I didn't expect Christmas to come so soon. At 4 a.m., we awoke to our parents' voices clamoring: "It's Christmas. Santa has come. Rise and shine. Merry Christmas! Get up. We're having Christmas!" Moments later, two excited children joined the grown-ups to open gifts. After opening presents, the adults figured they'd go back to bed as their best way to get some uninterrupted sleep.

There beneath the tree sat my table hockey game, the one with the metal rods that pulled in and out to skate the players on top of the painted-on ice. All day, the next week, all month, the following year and for years to come, I played that game. In fact, as a freshman in college, I drove home after the USA national team beat the Soviets in the 1980 Olympic Games. I went to the attic to find that game and took it back to our dorm. Eight overgrown boys played it nightly for three weeks in a round-robin tournament. As a child, I never received a gift that was more fun.

The only thing wrong with that Christmas Day was a goose that took too long to cook. At 7:30 p.m., Mom finally called us to the table. My sister and I, more exhausted than hungry and slumping in our chairs, were carted off to bed without tasting a bite. It was still the best Christmas ever.

I had no idea this would be the last Christmas we would celebrate together as a family. Life was about to change dramatically.

Rethink It

1. How has your childhood upbringing—your past—contributed positively or negatively to reaching your potential?

2. Are there parts of your childhood you'd say in some way held you back?

3. Is there a period in your childhood that had a significant impact on your sense of self-esteem? Describe that.

4. List any ways your sense of worth remains positively or adversely affected by those childhood events.

5. What are some things you can do to begin the process of correcting any unhealthy ways you think about yourself? For example, are there things you could do to try and replace doubt, fear and negativity with hope, positivity and belief?

CHAPTER FOUR

My World Turns Upside Down

You need to spend time crawling alone through shadows
to truly appreciate what it is to stand in the sun.

Shaun Hick, *The Army of Five Men*

In stark contrast to that Christmas holiday, the next fall my family fell apart. At twelve years old, I had never seen my parents fight, at least not with the passion they brought to a verbal argument in our living room one night. In a heated exchange, it was as if they forgot I was standing in the room. Days later, my mom, along with my sister and a few of their belongings, said a tearful good-bye and walked out the front door. I looked on, shocked with disbelief.

Perhaps my deformities added to some of my parents' stress? Maybe I should have felt responsible? To my recollection, I never did. I felt more like a victim. Instantly swept into a wave of chaos and confusion, I wrestled to understand circumstances that made no sense to me.

What I saw and perceived through my twelve-year-old eyes wasn't accurate or complete. I only knew that Mom had left our home. A few days later, she asked me to climb into the back seat of a car

31

driven by another "Bob." This "Bob" was not my father. The three of us had an outing on the beach that felt uncomfortable. Silently, I sat at a picnic table and picked at my food. Then, on the ride home, Bob reached out to take my mom's hand in his. My fears confirmed; my heart hardened. For years after that, I'd blame my mom (only and unfairly) for an event that caused me heartache and pain. Not until college would I accept that my dad, too, had made serious marital mistakes, and understand how hard Mom had worked to try and repair a relationship steeped in a history of challenges.

I only knew this—I hurt. My family as I'd known it was no more. I wanted things to be different—the same as they had been—but no amount of self-effort could fix circumstances beyond my ability to control.

My parents, kind and gentle souls at heart, remained amiable. They often talked about the needs of my sister and me. In fact, during some confusing and chaotic times for us all, on several occasions my mom moved back into our home. Each time, I hoped it would work. It never did, causing me to grow more discouraged. Young, angry and bitter, I started to lash out at both Mom and Bob (who eventually became my stepdad). Mom continued to reach out to me. But I felt as if my world had turned upside down.

There wasn't much about the situation that I liked. I was angry at my mom, yet I missed her greatly. Mom and my sister, Tami, lived in a tiny apartment about a mile from me during my seventh- and eighth-grade years. Although it was a short walk from school, I didn't like it and so I tried not to visit. But I'd often pout and wish my mom was with me.

If there was a silver lining, it was this: I remained in my house with my dad. Mom knew it would be tough for me to part from Dad, given our shared interest in sports. So sacrificially, she'd let me stay. Mostly, in evenings and on weekends I had Dad to myself, and that provided me some satisfaction.

Golf, Junior High and My Search to Belong

Once Mom left our home, Dad picked up his golf clubs after ten years of rarely having played. Within a year, he'd won a club championship and a regional event—with me "on his bag" as a caddy. About my seventh-grade year, he bought me a starter set of my own, and then he purchased us a membership at the local course. We practiced or played whenever we could.

Dad wasn't one to over-coach, so he let me wrap my hands around a golf club in a way that felt natural to me. The fingers of my right hand pinched the lower part of the grip just beneath those of my left. My right hand, grip pressure mostly light, was basically along for the ride. As I swung, I learned to use the stump of my left thumb to help slow and control my backswing at the top. Dad would only occasionally correct me, mostly focusing on the basics: ball position, body alignment, making a full shoulder turn—all fundamental techniques. With a few small changes, I kept my original grip. When Dad advised me to adjust something, I tried to do it, able to see how well he hit the ball and played.

Most summer days of my junior-high years, I pedaled my bicycle five miles from our home to the course. I draped my bag over my shoulder. Once at the course, I practiced and played all day. Each day, my enthusiasm grew when the time neared for Dad to show up from work. I filled his ears with my day's adventures, and we talked of the interesting people I'd played with or met. We hustled to get in as many holes as we could before dark. The next day would be the same routine.

Back then, I lacked the size and strength to drive a golf ball far, but I was pretty accurate, and my consistency improved. Dad praised me for my progress. One evening, we played the difficult right-dogleg, par-4 fifth hole of Toledo's Olalla Valley Golf Club, our home course. My second shot sailed past the spot where my dad's drive had finished. My chest puffed as I asked, "Dad, do you think someday I'll hit the golf ball as far as you?"

Silence ensued. The only sound I heard for several minutes was the echo of the "plunk" of our balls in the cup. Slowly, I trudged to the next tee. Dad called me to a bench, where he thrust his arm around me. He looked at me and said, "Son, I love you. I wish I thought it was possible. With your hands, I'm not sure it can happen." It was one of the very few times I can ever recall that Dad didn't believe I could do anything I set my mind to. He was just being honest, but my insides churned the rest of the round. I was discouraged that night as I climbed into my bed, but by the next morning the sting of the blow had faded. So I hoisted my clubs to my shoulder and pedaled to the course, determined to work harder at a game I loved.

School days, courses and activities like band, politics and team sports gave me a break from thinking about the realities of home.

All through junior high, I played drums, both the bass and snare. I'd mastered the five- and seven-beat rolls by ninth grade, but the band teacher forced me to choose: either play basketball or be part of the pep band. At 4'10" and ninety pounds, with a future career in the NBA, that choice was easy—even if today I have some regrets.

Toward the end of seventh grade, I decided to make a run at politics and campaigned for student body president. Politically wise beyond my experience, I chose Steve (Stretch—my bully-fighting buddy) to be my running mate. He was the most popular student on campus. With Steve's popularity, my self-created slogan—"Shouldn't you be votin' for Sto-ton"—and speeches packed full of empty promises, we won in a landslide victory. I led the Pledge of Allegiance to open school assemblies my eighth-grade year. I left no great legacy. Our committee (congress) never acted on anything. (We were ahead of our time!) Not much of a president, I nonetheless gained the respect of teachers who admired my determination and grit.

A good student, I made several trips from the bleachers to the stage to receive awards at our eighth-grade graduation assembly. I strutted to the stage to multiple ovations—none louder than that when Coach Newberry honored me as "Outstanding Physical Education Student." I'd broken physical barriers and exerted added effort in some academic work to be the top point-getter in Coach's merit-based system. That day my head just about popped from pride!

After school I'd play team sports, but I was no longer the star. The skills of peers taller and stronger were as good, if not better, than mine. I substituted, and didn't mind, on teams that lost only one game my seventh- through ninth-grade years. Mostly, I just felt the need to fit in and be accepted.

At one practice, a few of us scrubs were messing around in the gym before practice. Coach Newberry caught us, sent us to the showers, and later called us into his office to tell us that we were done—as in "cut" from the team. Acting as group spokesman, and tearing up some, I got out something like: "Coach, I don't even have to play in the games; just let me practice with the guys." By the next morning he'd had a change of heart. This craving to belong would lead me to make some poor choices by the time I went to college.

Goal-motivated

In the game of golf, in particular, I liked that I could set a scoring goal and then strive to achieve it. If I improved and managed to better that mark, I had a new goal to chase. Often, it took me longer than I wanted to shoot a lower score (and eventually I never could do better), but such "possibility thinking" always motivated and excited me. (It still does! Although today, I try to give thought to the motivation for why I've set a goal.)

Back then, even though my hands and feet were different, I didn't think of myself as a child born "handicapped." (There, of course, is nothing wrong with being born handicapped. I just didn't see myself that way.) Internally, I fought not to let others have that image of me. Setting goals helped me prove I was normal. Sometimes, a little like a greyhound dog chasing an electric bunny it can't catch around a circular track, I'd set a goal and work like a dog to achieve it, just wanting to make myself look good in the eyes of others. It took me decades to realize how the inner satisfaction of goals, once met, so quickly fades.

During my freshman year at Toledo High School, emotionally needy and wanting to feel good, I set some goals and triumphed. I learned to ride a unicycle forward in about three weeks. My timing to "perfect" the unicycle was ideal. School administrators that year let seniors initiate freshmen in a two-hour all-school assembly. I watched my peers get "egged," doused with garlic-scented liquid, and have their whiskers plucked, while all I had to do was keep pedaling— once more the center of everyone's attention, which I loved. Once I could pedal forward, I went hog wild trying to learn to pedal backward until one time I fell to the ground and about broke my neck. Riding backward was a goal I never met!

That year I also watched Dad make thirty-two consecutive free throws in our driveway. Impressed and in awe, I decided that I could make fifty consecutive shots from the fifteen-foot stripe. Mr. Hargett, our high school PE teacher, promised me a "50 Consecutive" T-shirt and a plaque with my name on the gym wall if I could do it. For weeks, I shot more than five hundred free throws a day. One morning, a shot that would have been my forty-eighth make in a row clunked off the back of the rim. Jeff, my friend, had faithfully rebounded for weeks. "Greg," he said, "I'm done. I'll go to a store and buy you a T-shirt." A few days later, with Jeff still faithfully beneath the rim, I made my fiftieth consecutive shot, and then six more, for fifty-six in a row. I would have tried to beat my mark, but Jeff had had enough.

My World Turns Upside Down—Again

Successes like these had helped me to once more find my stride. Best I could, I'd adapted to my parents' separation, with things going pretty well. But in the spring of my freshman year, I came home from school one day to see Grandma and Grandpa Stoughton seated on our living room sofa. My dad, anxious and severely depressed at mid-life, had walked himself into a treatment center. Wisely, he'd sought professional help. My heart felt as if a bomb had exploded within me—again.

At Grandpa and Grandma's suggestion, I lived with them that summer in Portland. Growing up, we'd often made the three-hour drive to their home to visit. I enjoyed Grandma, but in particular, Grandpa and I had grown close. He'd taken me as an apprentice on some of the odd jobs he'd worked as a handyman.

Great day of fishing with Grandpa

He'd taught me how to ride a bike, and shown me how to fish. (He baited my hook. I reeled them in—one morning catching nine rainbow trout to his three.) Whether we churned homemade ice cream, pitched yard darts (objects with sharp points tossed at circular targets, now banned) or went to minor league baseball games, I enjoyed the time we spent. But that summer felt different. With Dad ill, it was hard to be there.

Someone had arranged for me to play free golf. Like at home, I rode my bicycle to the course and played and practiced a lot. That summer, I shot a 78 one day, breaking 80 for the first time on a regulation course. But with Dad not there to see it (or cheer), the accomplishment didn't mean as much. Grandpa did the best he could in the role of surrogate father.

By August, Dad had recovered, and I was glad. The two of us were together again. But unbeknownst to me, I was about to have to navigate another bend in life's road.

Whiplash

Dad thought it best to get a fresh start, so he accepted a new position with the state of Oregon in Albany, a town about sixty miles east of Toledo. There, a pulp mill and a metal-processing plant bordered I-5, spewing fumes that earned the town of thirty thousand the nickname "The Armpit of Oregon." In comparison, Toledo seemed sweet-smelling. In spite of my protest, Dad bought a small home within walking distance of a large, newly built school.

South Albany High School was a maze of buildings with twelve hundred students I'd never before seen or met. I was lost in a crowd. No one knew me, or how well I'd overcome my deformities. No one cared about my past, what I'd faced at home, or what I'd done. I felt miserably alone. A "nobody," I desperately yearned to be a "somebody" again.

My adjustment to a new school was difficult, and then Dad gave me whiplash. "C'mon, son, we're driving to the coast," he said one night. First we went to a Toledo football game to hang with a few of my friends. But afterward, Dad drove us to Newport and introduced me to LaVerne, a woman he'd worked with in the past. Recently divorced, she had four daughters, including two teenagers at home.

39

Within months, around Christmas of 1976, my dad and my new stepmom wed. My world turned topsy-turvy again.

Issues of adjustment and dysfunction were present everywhere within our blended home. Once more chaos reigned. Unexpectedly, I found myself thrust into a battle for my dad's attention and love. With my "friendship" with Dad admittedly a bit too chummy and close, my stepmom and I waged war. I was flippant and she was volatile. Conflict became an unhealthy norm in the home. Even Dad and I learned to yell. My stepsisters and I shared a house, but with their activities wild and disturbing to me, we had little in common. Off-kilter and confused, I felt more lost than before.

Identity Gone

In Toledo, if life felt out of control I could turn to sports. However, at a larger school this source of my identity was gone. Too small to play football, I also got cut from the sophomore basketball team. Even though I wanted to hang with the "jocks," I quickly realized I couldn't. I was a "wanna-be" member of an overly elite group. Most days I walked the high school campus alone, ate lunch by myself, and struggled to fit in—lacking a place to earn merit and shine. Increasingly, I grew inwardly insecure.

I didn't golf well enough to be part of the clique, but my ability saved me some. In Toledo, as a freshman I'd played varsity golf, sometimes in the top spot. At South Albany, Dad had to beg the coach to let me be a part of the junior varsity squad. The coach took note of my work ethic, and I improved. By my senior year, I'd shot a 74 and 75 on consecutive days on a par-70 course to win two varsity tournaments. One day in practice I shot a 34, one-under-par and still my personal nine-hole best.

Journalism, too, helped a bit. Miss Bateman, a teacher of mine, thought I could write, so she recruited me to the school newspaper. Junior year I served as sports editor, and then senior year was editor of the paper. My teacher then worked some connections to land me a job as a sportswriter at the Albany Democrat-Herald, a daily newspaper of thirty-thousand readers.

Around that time, my dad taught me how to type. He coached me to divide the keys on the typewriter into two halves and then use one finger on each hand to plunk them. I used my right thumb to hit the space bar—a technique close to the "hunt and peck" system many people who never took typing use on computer keyboards today. Soon, I became fast enough to type information and quotes from coaches during telephone interviews that I'd then turn into sports stories.

During my junior year, Miss Bateman thought highly enough of me to nominate me for the Albany "Optimist Award." I won. It was nice, but I was more pessimistic inside than I ever cared to project. I put on a good front, but most days I still walked campus feeling glum.

Graduation and a Difficult Loss

On June 5, 1979, my eighteenth birthday, I graduated high school. Afterward, I went to a parent-organized all-night party, although I was in no mood to celebrate. The weekend prior, my grandparents had come to town for the big event. My stepmom and grandpa went deep-sea fishing in Newport. Grandpa Stoughton landed a large and impressive fish. Five minutes later, a smile still fresh on his face, he collapsed to the ship's deck and died from a massive heart attack. Days later, with no sleep, I slumped in the back seat of our car. Grandma Stoughton was in the front seat as we drove to Portland to pay our last respects to my grandpa. I'd lost a man I greatly admired and loved.

Life had ceased to be fun and games. So many uninvited and painful things had happened. With college looming, I'd sometimes think, *Maybe once I'm there, I can hit reset and enjoy life again.*

That September, Dad said good-bye at the curb of our home with an awkward hug and the words, "I love you; good luck." As I drove off, alone, in my faded-yellow Opel Kadett, my thoughts and emotions ran wild. On one hand, heading forty miles south to the University of Oregon, I had never felt more scared. On the other hand, seeing myself away from home—independent and free—I felt encouraged that a fresh start could lie ahead.

Rethink It

1. How did you experience "whiplash" growing up?

2. Are there ways you have sought to compensate for what you experienced as a child—especially for that which affected you beyond what you could control?

3. Is there something you did as a child that you'd say "defined" you then or defines you still today?

4. Is goal-setting a regular part of your life? Why or why not?

5. In what ways do the personal choices you make accentuate or minimize your perceived limitations?

CHAPTER FIVE

Restart My Way

How could youths better learn to live than by at once trying the experiment of living?

Henry David Thoreau, *Walden*

I checked into Oregon's Smith Hall and opened the door of room 306. Suitcase in hand, I peeked inside. Joe, my randomly assigned roommate, wasn't there, but his suitcase sat in the middle of the room. On the wall above the twin bed on the right was a poster that showed a skeleton of the human body and naming all its muscles. However odd, this told me Joe had marked his spot.

I dropped my suitcase and made a few trips to my car to gather the rest of my stuff. Then, following a couple of hours exploring campus, I opened the door and there stood Joe. My jaw dropped. I gawked at the sight of a 5'7" beast, his frame chiseled with muscles that bulged in places I didn't know muscles existed.

"Hi," Joe said, confidently stretching out his hand toward mine. "I'm Joe. It's nice to meet you." Sheepishly, I stuttered, "N-n-n-nice to meet you, too." We unpacked our bags and a little of our lives. Joe, a Hawaiian, was laid-back and relaxed. The son of a prominent and wealthy politician, he projected an air of self-assurance and confidence I knew I lacked. With little in common for us, Joe soon excused himself to head to a fraternity bash.

Meanwhile, I sat in the room and stared at the empty walls, on my own—alone again. On my drive to campus that morning, I'd made a vow: *Whatever it takes to be accepted and liked, that's what I will do. I will step out to be part of the crowd.* With that, I ambled down the hall, looking for activity. Moments later, my half-thumb and two fingers wrapped themselves around something new. I hoisted my first-ever can of cold beer. Licking my lips, I downed a few more until I was tipsy, if not drunk.

At age eighteen and on my own, I left home tentative yet ready to make it in a world entirely different and new. However, I was insecure, emotionally frail and of low self-worth. Within hours I'd become "that guy"—the poster child for *Here's how peer pressure works.* With a reckless first step, I had opened myself to a new lifestyle.

That first night I made a poor choice. That choice led to another bad decision, and then to another, in a new pattern of behavior that, had my parents known, would have rivaled their worst nightmare for me. Five nights that week I stumbled into my bed in a drunken stupor.

Freshman year classes started and I bought my books—Intro to Journalism, Microeconomics, US History and another course or two. Joe bought his and neatly stacked them on the corner of his desk. He never cracked the cover of a textbook our entire (nine-week) quarter together. I may have partied, but at least I did my schoolwork—even trying hard to glean something from the Monday, Wednesday, and Friday 8 a.m. economics lectures delivered to a crowd several hundred strong. I squeezed out a C- in that class—the only grade I ever received in college that wasn't an A or B.

Joe being savvy and me naïve, and with Joe in need of a few bucks, he asked me one evening, "Hey, Greg, do you play backgammon?" I never had. "I'll teach you how to play," he said. I won the first time I ever played. "You're really good," Joe said, feeding into my need for praise. "How about we put a couple dollars on this next game?" I lost game two. "Oh, you were just unlucky. Let's do it again—double or nothing." Four double-or-nothings later, and $16 in debt, I gained a life lesson and quit.

Seven weeks into the term, Joe came into our room one night, flashed open his wallet and asked, "Hey, would you like some baby powder?" My naïveté had its limits. Alcohol seemed okay, but I'd weighed in advance the risk and perils of doing hard drugs. Thinking it was cocaine—*because, if it were baby powder, why would I want it?*—I said, "No thanks." A week later, Joe entered our room high. He backed me into a corner and then, clutching a wad of my shirt in his hands, lifted me two inches off the ground. "I don't like you very much," he said. The feeling was mutual by then. Joe flunked out of college later that year—but right then, I figured it was a good time to find a new roommate and move.

New Friends and Mom

I got reassigned to a room downstairs with Jay, a pre-med student I enjoyed, on a floor of more quality guys. I'd met one of these guys,

47

Mike, my first day on campus. We noticed one another's golf clubs when we registered for our rooms, pledging to play together.

Mike was warm and friendly, and more reserved in nature than me. A student in pre-dentistry, he, too, studied a lot. But when winter gave way to spring, Mike was eager to break for some golf. We played several times. I pounded my clubs into the ground and cursed my way up the fairways and around the greens after every bad shot. Mike, slightly better than me, kept his cool, never saying a word, somehow able to tolerate my abrasiveness.

Whenever Mike drove us to and from the course, he slipped a cassette of Christian music into the player. I never cared, just seeing it as something important to Mike. The guys on the floor had grown used to his different ways. He attended church on Sundays and went to Bible studies and Friday-night gatherings of a Christian club. At meals I saw him close his eyes and dip his head in what seemed a brief prayer. Mike was Mike, and I liked Mike.

Mike's roommate, Mark, was different than Mike that year. Several of us had on occasion joined Mark in the back of "Woody," his beat-up van, to drink. That was freshman year. On the first evening of sophomore year, Mark and I walked a mile to the front door of a fraternity bash. Suddenly, Mark stopped. "Greg," he said, "I can't do this. I can't go inside." Taken aback, I replied, "What? Why?" On our way home, Mark told me how he'd made some changes that summer, entering into a relationship with Jesus. Like Mike, Mark wasn't one to force anything on me. I gave it thought on my own for a few weeks—but in no mood to change, it wasn't something I wanted to do.

Freshman year, when things felt hard, I started to initiate more contact with Mom.

Mom and my stepdad had taken my verbal "shots" as a teenager and not fired back. I knew they loved me and felt bad that my sister and I had been hurt. The geographic separation from my sister then is a factor in a relationship that remains a bit distant. But by my ninth grade year, Mom and Bob had moved to Central Oregon, and I started to make more trips east over Oregon's Cascades mountain range to visit. As Mom and I caught up, I found that I liked my stepdad, Bob. He was a playful guy—a big kid at heart—who liked to tease. I enjoyed being with them, though I didn't know what to make of Mom's renewed commitment of faith. She and Bob went to church on Sundays. She talked about how she'd been forgiven in Jesus. I heard it, yet to me it didn't make sense. They invited me to join them and never forced me to attend, but I could tell it pleased Mom when I tagged along. On several occasions, I did.

At school, I'd phone Mom, panicked. Before midterms and final exams, I lived with fear that no matter how hard I studied, I'd likely fail. The thought of doing so put knots in my stomach. I craved Mom's voice of calm reassurance. "You'll do fine," she'd say. "I'm praying for you." I'd phone again to tell her of my A or B and to hear her say, "I told you so. Great job."

Jobs, Dates and More Roommates

Other than summer break and to work at the golf course, I didn't go home to Albany much during my college years. When I did, I had a room and a bed; however, my relationship with my stepmom remained tense. Talks with Dad would remind me of my need to get

49

back to school, make money and work. (With my own son now in college, it makes sense!) Dad provided for my basic needs, but we hadn't saved enough. So I worked twelve to twenty hours a week all four years on campus to help pay my way through school.

I started at the bottom—literally—in the basement of a dormitory cafeteria. I'd don a parka and enter a large storage freezer. There I would knife and peel away the plastic wrap of institutional-size packages of frozen meat. I hated the corned beef hash with its awful, uncooked stench, so I was thankful when I soon moved up. I loaded a truck with food prepared in our kitchen and then delivered it to a nearby cafeteria. By the end of my sophomore year, I advanced to dishwasher and some hours on the dining room floor. By junior year, I had amassed enough seniority to work fifteen to twenty hours per week as a roster checker. It was the university's system (pre-computers) to try and keep students and their friends from mooching meals. Seated in front of a giant-size board—with a list of students' names—I placed a check by a person's name each time they entered the cafeteria to eat.

At the roster, I learned names. In particular, I remembered the names of the gals who ate there. Calling them by name made some of them feel known, and they were impressed. Others seemed more creeped out by it. It did give me a leg up to initiate discussions with girls I found attractive. However, I was a one-date wonder. Girls polite, sympathetic or compassionate enough to say "yes" to a first date with me never seemed as interested the next time I asked. If I developed feelings for one but was turned down, I'd agonize on my bed with no clue what to say or do. Dating for me was awkward, confusing and hurtful.

I had always felt there was nothing I couldn't do. I might not do it as well as others, but I could do anything. Somehow, that didn't seem to be true when it came to trying to move from dates to a relationship. I felt certain I'd never have a girlfriend or find a wife. I thought my physical imperfections were to blame when it was my social skills, habits and character that needed work. Eventually, I figured it out.

At school and content with my job at the roster, I lived in the dorms all four years. My junior year I negotiated a larger, corner room in Carson Hall. In need of a roommate, I turned toward Mike. Surprisingly, he agreed. I liked Mike's easygoing nature. The fact that he studied away from our room and ran with a different crowd also made it easy for us to do a few things together. (I didn't get on his nerves too much.)

I watched Mike with more intrigue than he knew when he read his Bible and prayed. Some Sundays he invited me to church. If not hung over, I sometimes went. It was something to do. Later I would say, "Thanks, Mike, for taking me to church. Say, I'm thinking of having a party in our room. Do you mind?" He was okay with it. "If that's what you want to do," he'd say. "It's your room, too." As the music blared louder and the antics grew wilder, I'd ask, "Where's Mike?" Quietly, he'd slipped away.

At the end of that school year, Mike transferred to dental school in Portland. So I asked a guy named Tom to room with me my senior year. The year before, I'd liked Tom's study habits, and we'd had some good talks. But Tom returned from the summer a changed man. Our room was home to some scary parties, and Tom's bad choices, vulgarity and immaturity grew to repulse me. By graduation, I'd come full circle. I had a roommate I thought even less of than Joe.

Welcome to Advertising Media

I wanted to leave the University of Oregon in four years with a degree, but some moments I wasn't sure I would. I'd gotten good grades, but I lacked focus for my future. I didn't know what to pursue for a career. In my freshman year, I'd decided not to become a sportswriter due to the late nights and low pay. During sophomore year, I tried computer science and realized I was technologically inept. I wandered into history and enjoyed it, but I didn't see where it would take me. Then in the fall of my junior year, a lousy professor and a hideous small-group experience ruined marketing for me. By the second quarter of my junior year, I felt confused and in trouble.

An advisor suggested I try advertising, so I enrolled in Advertising Media. I got to class early the first day, elbowed the guy next to me, and said, "This course sounds like a piece of cake." He shot me a glance and replied, "I don't think so; I've heard it's pretty tough." The door closed, and a pair of well-shined shoes clicked on the tile floor as they passed. At the front of the classroom, a professor turned for the reveal. A chic thirty-something guy in a dapper three-piece suit said, "Hi, welcome to Advertising Media. My name is Bob Taber."

Bob greeted us kindly enough, sharing a personal bio that included some recent ad agency experience. "Let's get to know one another," he said, launching us into a "name game." I elbowed my seatmate and whispered, "See, this guy's cool." Then Bob turned corporal. "This will be the most difficult class you'll take in the program," he said.

"Look to your right. Look to your left. Only one of the three of you will be here after the first exam. Those still here can expect to pull two consecutive all-nighters on a final project. Last semester, I gave one A." He continued on until, mercifully, the bell sounded.

Sweat poured from my brow. My insides quaked. My last gasp for a college degree felt gone. Bob walked past me and out the door. Afraid and dejected, I rose to my feet. *What do I do now?* My legs carried me down the hallway and to the door of the office into which Bob had ducked. Awkwardly, I gawked from the edge of the door as he circled his desk, sat and shuffled some papers. At last, he looked up to see me and asked, "Would you like to come in?" Sporting a deer-in-the-headlights look, I slumped into a chair across from his desk and babbled a few details of my life and educational journey. Patiently, he listened. He then talked me off the ledge. "Greg," he concluded, "I think you should give it a try."

Everything Bob had said of the course was true. I passed the brutal midterm. I pulled two straight all-nighters on a project. I didn't get the A. I earned a B+, good enough for me to continue my pursuit of an advertising degree.

Bob called me the next fall to come and meet in his office. He asked if I would lead a small team to submit a project in a national advertising competition sponsored by Philip Morris. The next four months, three of us worked feverishly to develop a campaign for Oregon Freeze Dry Foods, a subsidiary of the tobacco company. Our project proposed that the Oregon firm take its dehydrated products, used by astronauts and backpackers, and put them on supermarket shelves. We named the product "Entrée Vite"—or "quick meal" in

French—with a campaign slogan of "Great Taste Doesn't Take Time." (That was a lie; the food was awful.) But being the marketers we were, I opened my mailbox one day in April to find a Mailgram that read: "Congratulations, your product has been judged first place nationally of ninety colleges and universities." Once again, I'd achieved something about which I could feel proud.

A month later, we boarded a plane for an all-expenses-paid trip to New York City. There we presented our project to corporate executives and got a tour of Manhattan, highlighted by a swanky party atop one of the twin towers of the World Trade Center, which then stood tall. In search of a job, I'd faxed a copy of the Mailgram to several 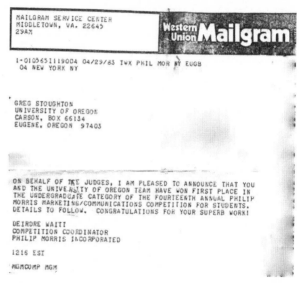 agencies in San Francisco that I'd interviewed with that spring with no callbacks. Upon my return from New York, there were messages (pink slips) from agencies taped all over my dorm room door. A week later, I flew to San Francisco for a second round of interviews with Foote, Cone and Belding Advertising. Days later, while visiting Grandma Stoughton, I took a phone call to accept an offer.

A few evenings before commencement, I celebrated as heartily as I had in my freshman days. Though I'd matured some, too many weekends I'd lived for the thrill of the moment—for a temporal "high" that I thought would pacify my inner ache. Yet like sports or achievements, the highs I felt—these more

At graduation with my dad and stepmom

dangerous—didn't last or fulfill. Looking back, I was fortunate, spared of potentially devastating consequences from some decisions that lacked sound judgment. And now with regret, I'd have liked to have spent more time with a different crowd, and to have had more fun than I did.

Positively, college offered me the chance to prove I could make it on my own—but with a mixed bag of results. On one hand, I'd failed miserably. In search of acceptance and significance, I'd sold out and done things I'd never before considered. On the other hand, I could see a trickle of personal growth.

Through achievement, I'd recovered some of my prior self-confidence and grit. I'd earned a degree and landed a promising job. In this, my façade projected optimism. However, on the inside I could think, *Maybe Mom does know best.* I knew she felt horrified that her little boy would soon walk the streets of the big city—San Francisco—and encounter still more of this world.

Rethink It

1. Have you ever chosen to follow the crowd or coerced someone else to act according to the ways of a group you were part of?

2. What can you do to minimize the impact of peer pressure or "group think" on how you believe, think or act?

3. When would you say group think is harmful or unhealthy? Do you think there are ways group think can be helpful or beneficial?

4. How has peer pressure positively or adversely affected your ability to unleash your potential?

5. What, if any, changes do you want to make in how you believe, think or act as a result of reading this chapter and considering these questions?

CHAPTER SIX

Culture Shock

Yesterday ended last night.

John C. Maxwell, *The 15 Invaluable Laws of Growth*

San Francisco is only 750 miles from Toledo, Oregon. However, the exquisite City by the Bay felt like a galaxy far, far away compared to the dainty, tightly knit community where I had grown up as a boy. I exchanged a view of a smokestack for Victorian homes, a towering skyline, the Golden Gate Bridge and people everywhere—many of whom struck me as different, if not downright strange.

I encountered people radically unlike me, nothing like people I'd been around before. In the late 1960s, Oregon Governor Tom McCall had drawn fire from Californians when he said, "You're welcome to visit; just don't stay." While I liked the multicultural city, some of what I observed gave credibility to the governor's thinking about the state to the south. It struck me as a land of crazies of all kinds. From outrageous hairstyles and body painting to bizarre clothes (or no clothes at all, like the guy who welcomed me to the city with a "flash"!), I was horrified. Forget Oz, Dorothy! In San Francisco, she would have definitely known she wasn't in Kansas anymore.

At the University of Oregon, I'd earned my degree. However, still naïve, I'd not journeyed far from freshman year and the night Joe schooled me on the backgammon board. I hadn't given much thought to some things—for instance, homosexuality. I had no clue that San Francisco even then was its epicenter in America.

Fresh out of college, and needing to bank some bucks, I graciously accepted the offer of a relative of mine to move into his—and his roommate's—small Victorian home located in the "Castro District." I had no interest in their gay lifestyle and received no pressure from them to convert. But walking the Castro neighborhood opened my eyes to even more sights I hadn't encountered before—cross-dressers, prostitutes and rampant displays of public affection. If college had ushered me into the real world, San Francisco exposed me to culture shock new and extreme.

My First "Real" Job

Outside Castro, there was much about San Francisco and the Bay Area that I liked. A resplendent city of two bridges on a bay, with the Pacific Ocean a short Muni (Metro) ride away, the Bay Area's beauty never lost its sheen to me. Its bedroom communities of Sausalito and Tiburon backed up to magnificently beautiful hills of grass. Sausalito was a short ferry ride away. The view back across the bay of Transamerica's pyramid building and a magnificent city landscape exceeded even the fantastic food I ate.

Weekday mornings exhilarated me. My heart pulsed when I popped up from the underground to join the chorus of heels that paraded down the street. Even on brisk days, my London Fog jacket buttoned tightly, a fifteen-minute walk up Sansome Street caused my adrenaline to pump, and my pace was brisk. Swept into urgency as part of the crowd, I felt important, if not significant.

Foote, Cone and Belding Advertising sat nestled against the backdrop of San Francisco's Telegraph Hill, with Coit Tower visible above. I arrived at the agency my first day, took one last deep breath, and then flung open its front door. Believing I looked sharp in my new suit, I sought to project an air of self-confidence. A few steps inside and I spotted the Senior Media Director. My eyes met his gaze. Assertively, I stretched out my arm and fingers, our handshake imminent. At the last moment, he pulled back his hand. "Welcome," he said. "Now, let me help you." While my soon-to-be-peers looked on, the big boss circled behind me to tuck in a shirt collar that poked out from the neck of my jacket. Embarrassed, I felt a mess.

Earlier that morning, I recalled that I couldn't yet button the top button of my dress shirt by myself. I hadn't yet learned to do what seemed a difficult if not impossible task, so I'd shaken my uncle's mattress to wake him up and ask him to fasten my button. I did the same thing each morning my first three weeks on the job. Until one evening I got home, looked in the mirror, and got mad. *Enough!* My fingers fumbled at the collar, trying a variety of techniques. Forty-five minutes later, shocked and excited, I'd buttoned my shirt. Swiftly, I undid the button to try it again. Twenty minutes later, it happened a second time. On my third try, I got it in five minutes. I've buttoned the top button of my dress shirt ever since, most times in a minute or less and free of any help.

Fortunately, my clothing snafu at work didn't matter. I'd made a good first impression with agency leaders and some of the staff when

I interviewed in May. I scored on answers to questions like: "If you were an airplane, which part would you be, and why?" and "What animal in a zoo is most descriptive of you?" I wowed them enough with my creative responses to land my media job.

On my prior visits to the agency, I'd seen lots of the office space, but somehow I'd missed the storage cave. The agency was tight on rooms, with plans to make a corporate move, so I started my career in a 3' x 6' closet with a desk. There, looking at a wall, I sat and worked. I didn't mind. I thought it cool to have my own private cubby.

Between the energy of the city, my responsibilities, and what I thought was a good salary of $16,000, I felt fulfilled—at first. Notebooks under my desk housed client budgets in excess of $12 million for Epson Computers, The Clorox Company, the California Raisin Advisory Board (CALRAB) and added clients.

In our work with CALRAB, a Creative Director had the idea to pair Marvin Gaye's hit song—"I Heard It Through The Grapevine"—with caricatures of raisins that danced. I envied his creative role. *Why couldn't I come to work at 11 a.m., coffee mug in hand and holes in my faded blue jeans to provide that one great idea worth a $150,000 salary?* His work, of course, was more challenging than I pictured. But with my nose to the grindstone, I helped support his idea. I allocated millions of dollars to a mix of print ads and TV commercials in developing CALRAB's 1985 media plan. I thought my plan could help sell lots of raisins and learned in the process that I wasn't too fond of numbers. I'd gravitated to media as much through my relationship with my professor, Bob—his compliments genuine and sincere—as I had for any interest in media.

Performing to People-Please

In my eighteen months with the agency, I had several bosses. My favorite was my first boss, Barbara. She was pleasant, likeable and fun. Clearly a talented person, her hard work and long hours had helped her advance through the ranks. Barbara was also a quick study of people. In no time, she knew how best to motivate me. She praised me for everything I did and then gently guided me to correct whatever needed to be fixed. I couldn't complete enough work quickly enough to satisfy my desire to please her and receive more of her praise.

It didn't take long for my hours to mirror Barbara's. I worked late nights and many weekends, too, and began to wonder: *When do I spend the money I make?* Nonetheless, I netted a great six-month review, according to Barbara the best she'd ever given. But with the bar set high, I grew anxious. Paralyzed by fear, I wondered if I could continue to meet some phantom expectations I held.

I didn't get it then; I couldn't see it yet. But I had this longing to perform and to people-please—a character flaw, deeply ingrained. Like professional athletes I'd idolized in my youth, their esteem only as secure as their last shot or win, I was equally fragile. This wasn't Barbara's fault. It wasn't my parents' fault. Powerful role models and major sources of encouragement like Coach Newberry and Professor Bob weren't to blame. In sports, school and work, breaking barriers, achieving and people-pleasing, I was like a dog rewarded after every new trick and eager to demonstrate more.

61

A second boss—another Barbara—did her best to fix a problem we didn't know I had. This Barbara managed with "the stick," and never "the carrot." I don't think she believed in the words "well done." Three consecutive Monday mornings I walked into my office to see her seated at my desk, rifling through a project of mine and looking up to say, "Good morning. Why did you do it this way? This isn't right." My psyche, accustomed to the other direction, took a hit.

Bill wasn't one of my bosses, yet within a few weeks I'd met him, the agency's Chief Operating Officer. It was a regular practice of his to walk the halls on breaks and visit with employees, especially those who were new. One day he stuck his head into "the cave" to introduce himself and say hello. Cordial, relaxed and never in a hurry, he would invite me to lunch some days. By the questions he asked, I could tell that Bill wanted to know me personally. He didn't care about my work. One day he asked, "What's your spiritual background?" Here we go again, I thought. I told him about those I'd met in college and of my mom's return to faith. Politely, he shared his story. Politely, I listened, trying to discern what he'd found so appealing in his "faith." *How is this Jesus from two thousand years ago relevant to me today? It's made a difference in his life? How can that be? Why do these people persist in sharing this message with me?* I didn't mind, as I appreciated Bill's personable and relational nature.

I'm Sick, and I Need to Go Home

In a city of culture shock, the world of big-city advertising had its share of jaw-dropping moments and events. These fed my desire to fit in, feel accepted and be liked.

After three weeks at the agency, I moved from the cave to share an office with Sam. (Perhaps they hoped I'd be of some positive influence.) Sam cussed like a drunken sailor and laid down a challenge. Which of us could curse the most on phone calls in one day? I wanted Sam to invite me for drinks with his group of peers after work, so—crazily—I agreed to compete. I cared more about what Sam thought of me than I did about my job, the reputation of our firm, and the people on the other end of the phone—some of them agency clients. I lost. I had no chance given Sam's foul mouth, but I got Sam's invite. At city bars, the alcohol flowed. In these settings, and at some agency parties, I didn't just drink. Plenty of evenings I went home full-on drunk, thinking it was good that I belonged.

Wednesday, September 14, 1983, the agency hosted an office cruise on the bay. I have a vague recollection of it being an unseasonably warm fall night, lights of the city reflecting atop the water. We circled Alcatraz Prison, eerily symbolic of my imprisoned state. Once back at the dock, I staggered from the boat and then weaved uptown a couple miles to a co-op at California and Webster Streets I'd called "home" since August.

The next day, two acquaintances of mine from Oregon came to the city for interviews. We met up after work and started the evening at a small room they had rented for a night. Seated on a couple of mattresses, we passed a pint, talked and stared out a window at the brick wall of another building three feet away. Tipsy, we taxied to a nightclub in the Marina District, close to the Golden Gate Bridge. There, on my knees in a restroom, miserably ill, I told them to go and I'd find my way home. For the next several hours, I staggered once more through San Francisco's streets. Once home, I collapsed onto my bed for a mostly sleepless night—instead busily making trips to the toilet and sink.

My alarm clock sounded loudly and early the morning of Friday, September 16. My head pounded and my body ached. Stomach churning, I showered, dressed and made it to work. I sat at my desk, but I didn't stay long. Nauseated, my body screamed. I knew I couldn't make it through a day's work. Eyes surely bloodshot, my body fatigued, I slumped into a chair in (the first) Barbara's office. "I'm sick," I said. "I have the flu; I need to go home."

Rethink It

1. How have you experienced "culture shock" due to a major life transition or some dramatic change in your circumstances?

2. What's your normal response to circumstances or situations that cause you to feel less in control?

3. In general, how comfortable are you with change?

4. How much have achievements, accomplishments, and accolades been part of you trying to define who you are and your sense of identity and worth?

5. What are a few lessons you've learned as a result of having made it through "culture shock" experiences?

6. What would you say if someone asked, "What's your spiritual background?" Has faith helped you to navigate change? How?

Note: If you are involved in any potentially harmful or addictive behaviors, I'd encourage you to find someone you feel you can talk to about your struggles.

CHAPTER SEVEN

Restart God's Way

There is no better news than the fact that Jesus can actually turn a life upside down and save it.

Cliff Richard, British pop singer

I had just lied to my boss. In no condition to work, I packed my items and left the office. I walked toward the Metro. The quiet of the midday streets first spoke to my conscience, dank and confused. I boarded a train and sat, alone and deep in thought.

An image of my dad flashed in my mind. I'd come to see some chinks in his armor. He wasn't as perfect as I once thought him to be, yet I knew he would never have done as I did. Only twice had I seen my dad with a beer. His example and ways were a severe contrast to my reckless pattern of behavior. *My life is headed nowhere in a hurry*, I thought. The turmoil within seemed to beg me to change. I wondered: *How will I do it?*

I opened the door to my room in the co-op, shed my shoes, and then plopped on my bed to rest. I wanted to sleep, but my mind wouldn't let me. *What am I missing? Is there something I lack that I just don't get? Can I—will I—change? And if so, how will that happen? What do I need to do?*

In recent weeks, I'd partied more, about as I'd done during my initial weeks of college. As I thought about my drinking, though, it seemed more rooted in an issue of my heart. I cared more about being liked than I did for the alcohol I consumed. I just didn't stop as a result of the acceptance I felt from others.

My mind drifted toward Bill—his friendliness and our recent conversations. I thought of Mark, of Mike, and of a consistency and calm—a peace—in their lives that I definitely admired. *Is it their faith?*

During my senior year of college, I'd opened my dorm door after a knock to see Jeff, a polite, twenty-something fellow gazing at me. "Hi Greg," he said, with a slight Texan drawl. "Mike thought I might drop by for a visit." That day, and then on a second occasion, Jeff, a pastor of the church Mike attended, walked me through a little booklet called, *Would You Like to Know God Personally?* (Appendix A, page 129).

In the booklet, Jeff drew my attention to its four main points:

1. God loved me and offered a wonderful plan for my life.

2. But I was sinful and separated from God. Therefore, I could not know and experience God's love and plan for my life. My sins were described to me as my thoughts, attitudes and actions that missed God's mark of perfection. These had made fellowship (relational intimacy) with God, my Creator, impossible.

3. Jesus Christ was God's only provision for my sin, and through Him I could know and experience God's love and plan for my life. Jesus, crucified on a cross, was "the way, and the truth, and the life" (John 14:6), and his death was the way for me to be forgiven for my sins. Buried, he had been raised from the dead to appear before witnesses—now seated with God in heaven, and alive.

4. It wasn't enough to know this intellectually. I'd need to receive Jesus Christ into my heart. By faith through prayer, I'd have to invite Him into my heart to become my personal Savior. By doing so, I could know and experience God's love and plan for my life.

During the times Jeff talked with me, my mom's words to me as a young boy had led me to believe that God exists: *You just tell them it's the way God made you.* The whiff of stale beer in my room affirmed that my life now reeked of sin—even if I couldn't yet recognize my bitterness and pent-up anger as proof that I'd been *born wrong.* It wasn't about my deformities; I'd been *born wrong* in a nature I'd inherited, called "sin." And I could reason it true that Jesus had come to Earth; my calendar each day was marked by the year A.D. (anno domini, Latin for "in the year of our Lord") that seemed evidence enough that Jesus had lived.

But what about this talk of his death and resurrection? What was I to do with that? It seemed a stretch. Jeff had offered historical evidence that I reckoned could be possible, maybe even true, but when asked to make a personal commitment, I said, "No. I can't do that." A lifestyle change seemed too great a sacrifice, so twice I politely sent Jeff on his way to talk to others instead.

A year later, my mind and my heart warred within. I wanted change, but could I take Jeff's suggested step? *What would it mean? What would I have to give up?*

God, have you not long pursued my soul? I thought, too, of Mom, and of Aunt Jean and Uncle Mike. (Years later, I would hear how my aunt and uncle interrupted family meals to pause and pray for me. Had those prayers helped bring me to this point?) *How many times had some teacher, coach or friend made some passing comment about their faith?* God, like a hound of heaven, seemed after me. *Why, God? Why me? Why now?*

Sure, my mom had made her mistakes. Weren't her ways contrary for years to Yours, God? She claims forgiveness. Is that where she gets her joy and peace? If I were to make this decision, could You really relieve my guilt?

I should call my mom. On the phone that day, Mom listened to me as I told her the details of my night. We didn't talk long, and she didn't say much. But what she said hit home. "Son, I've been praying for you," she said. "I love you. I'm sorry for some things that have made life hard for you, and it hurts to know that things right now are difficult. However, I believe you know what you need to do."

I hung up the phone and walked down the hall into my room. Once more, I dropped to my bed—this time, to give her words thought.

But what of Jesus' resurrection—that He'd been buried and brought to new life? Could I trust that? Had anything changed in my thoughts? Nothing had. (It would be a few years before I'd hear of a guy named Josh McDowell. Once a major skeptic, he'd spent seven years trying to disprove that event. He gave up, placed his belief in the Lord, Jesus Christ, and wrote two books on the topic from his findings: *More than a Carpenter* and *Evidence That Demands a Verdict*.) On that day in San Francisco, God hadn't erased all my doubts.

Nonetheless, September 16, 1983, a little before noon, I sat up, looked skyward and prayed:

> *"God, my life isn't going so well. I'm making a mess of things. I know I'm not living as You would want me to. Something is missing, and I think that something is You. My mom, my friends—they talk about Jesus as if He's real. I still have my doubts, but I'm going to, by faith, pray and receive Him. Jesus, come into my heart and forgive me of my sins. Change my life and help me become the person I think You would want me to be. If You are real, it would be a great time to show up. I'm ready to give this Christian life a try. Amen."*

Silently I pondered: *What happened? What have I done?* No trumpets blared; no fireworks exploded. I didn't hear Handel's "Hallelujah Chorus," feel tingly or begin to glow. My hands didn't sprout additional fingers; my feet grew no toes. Even the nausea of my heavy drinking didn't fade away right then. But a genuine sense of calm seemed to sweep over my disturbed and troubled heart. Something within me had changed.

One thing sure hadn't changed. Physically, I felt starved! I'd met a guy named Robert at the co-op where we both lived. Several times a day he would pass through my room to get to his. He was in, and he was hungry as well, so the two of us went to lunch. Over a meal, I told Robert about my new experience. My enthusiasm unconstrained, I recounted all that had happened in the past forty-eight hours. I told him about my prayer and about how different I felt. I told him I believed that God had come into my heart to help change my life. Robert listened politely, and then sort of sent me on my way—about like what I had done to Pastor Jeff and to Mike, Mark and others for years.

An Introduction to "Grace"

Earlier that week, I had decided I'd leave the co-op and the city. With my Friday afternoon free, and looking for a new place to live, I boarded a commuter bus to ride north across the Golden Gate Bridge to the community of San Rafael. On that ride, the bus stopped across from a church. Silently, I pledged to God that I would attend service there on Sunday. Two days later, I hopped from the bus, walked across a lot, looked skyward once more and prayed—best I knew how: *Okay, God, I'm doing this. No Mike. No Pastor Jeff. No Mom telling me I need to go to church. It's You and me here. Let's go.*

I opened the doors of Valley Baptist Church to a kind welcome from a gentleman who smiled, offered a firm handshake and escorted me to a Sunday school classroom upstairs. Still queasy about what I'd just done, I met (another) Bill. This Bill, a guy in his early twenties, was the teacher of a twenty-somethings group. Through conversation, Bill learned that I had no car. "I'm your wheels, Greg," he said.

"Shopping, rides to and from church—whatever you need—you let me know. I'll be there for you." And he was!

It took six more months for me to save enough money to purchase a car. Meanwhile, ever faithful, Bill kept his word. He drove me everywhere. In our travels, I found a genuine and caring friend. Bill embraced my deformities as well as my personality quirks.

On Sundays, Bill would drive by my apartment, and I would ride with him to church. I felt better when I went, so I attended regularly—even if sometimes it was a bit out of "duty." I did what felt right, even if my heart wasn't in it (except that I didn't go to Bill's "study group"). I felt insecure in what I knew about the Bible. Bill's authenticity and caring persistence kept me going to church, and learning a bit, at a time when my commitment was more social in nature. Today, I'm thankful for that.

I came to God and Jesus in need of a life change. At once, I quit cursing. That wasn't too hard for me to do, though it disappointed my coworker, Sam. But about three weeks after I'd made my commitment of faith, I went to a party with a roommate where I once more went home drunk. I awoke hung over, my conscience ridden with guilt. So that morning, I walked a mile to the church. I poured out my heart to a pastor named Ken, uncertain of what might happen next. *Would he boot me from the church? Would he say I didn't belong?* Neither of those things happened.

Instead, Ken introduced me to a word and a new concept. He talked to me about God's amazing "GRACE"—made clear to me by the acronym God's Riches at Christ's Expense. Freely, in Christ, through God's unmerited favor, He'd sent His Son to die for me.

Gaining His forgiveness had come from nothing I'd earned or deserved. In His love and acceptance of me, God forgave. "Greg, I can tell you feel badly about what you've done," Ken said. "God loves you, and He forgives you. He won't turn on you, or abandon you. How about if we thank God for that in prayer? Let's thank Him for forgiveness and ask for His strength—and then you move on."

I'm confident that Ken's choice that day to lovingly bless, and not condemn, helped free me forever from the abuse of alcohol. I had no idea that the next few decades I'd have to weave so much "grace" into the fabric of my life. For the moment, it had been an immediate and pleasant introduction.

Farewell, San Francisco

By the end of 1983, I'd picked up some basics of the faith from the lead pastor's teaching. So on Super Bowl Sunday of 1984, I took a dip in the baptismal pool, seeing it as a next step in obedience. (Silently, I voiced a prayer for my dad.)

At work, I'd taken a stand against peer pressure. To refrain from the temptation of alcohol, I opted not to be around it whenever possible. I'd made a few friends in the church. Now sober at office parties, I felt a disgust I had previously missed. These were mostly "meat markets" for employees who, once drunk, paired up. My heart for big-city advertising had begun to wane. Even the monthly bounce from reports of increased sales of Clorox bleach and raisins no longer excited me the way it once had.

I'd also grown weary of the city. With the forty-five-minute commute each way and long days at the office, I got home at 8 p.m. most nights. I then woke at 5:30 a.m. to do it all over again. Apart from occasional rounds of golf, a professional baseball game, church or an outing with friends, my time was scarce to enjoy the city, relax and have much fun. *Why am I doing this? Is big-city advertising for me? Is this what I want for my future? Is there something of greater significance—something else I might pursue?*

Thanksgiving of 1984, I phoned Dad to tell him I planned to quit and return to Albany and home. Disappointed, he advised me not to pass up the opportunity I'd been given. This time, I didn't do as he said. I told my new boss, Art, of my intent to resign at the end of the year. He asked me to take a day to go play golf and think about it. I did. It was a great day. I drove the ball well, shot an 81 and grew certain in my resolve to leave.

Humorous now but hurtful then, I gleaned an invaluable life lesson my final day at the agency. Arrogantly, I arrived that day thinking, *Wow, this place is going to miss me and all that I'm responsible for.* I entered my office to find a young woman I knew seated at my desk. She snagged a binder of mine that contained the records of one of the half-dozen accounts I'd worked. She flipped through the book and asked a good question or two. She moved to the next binder and then the next. By 3 o'clock that afternoon, she had command and control of what needed to be done. I was given an early farewell. I shook my head at the sham of my perceived significance and pride. That easily, I was replaced. Humbled a bit, I slumped out the door for my final commute.

Dad and I talked on the phone. We negotiated for me to live at home for a month. He reasoned it was time enough for me to figure out life's next chapter. In Albany, I'd come back to a place of security and comfort.

In San Francisco, I'd matured some. For eighteen months, I'd made it on my own—most significantly, leaving a path of destructive behavior to walk a better road. I had said "yes" to God and a relationship with Him, and I had taken a first step on my spiritual journey. I didn't yet know the magnitude of the choice I had made.

At age twenty-three, I felt better about myself, yet in some ways I remained idealistic and naïve. What I didn't know was this: In San Francisco, I'd gained "just enough" of what I needed to qualify my move to Oregon as a transition of God's intent. This move would profoundly change the direction of my life.

Rethink It

1. In what ways have you identified with my story?

2. Have there been a times in your life when you've asked questions such as: *What am I missing? What is it my heart lacks? Can I—will I—change? And if so, how will it happen? What do I need to do?*

Blaise Pascal, a French mathematician and philosopher, once wrote: "There is a God-shaped vacuum in the heart of every man, which cannot be filled by any created thing, but only by God the Creator, made known through Jesus Christ."

3. Are there ways that you've sought to fill an "empty heart" that haven't worked? (Buying something new? A new job? A promotion? Relationships? Other ways?) Write or share your thoughts.

4. Have past choices, missteps or failures left you feeling guilty? Do you believe God is capable and willing to forgive and wipe away those things? If so, will He? Has He? On what basis?

See Appendix A, page 129, for more insight on how God can forgive you and help you to move past your flaws and limitations.

CHAPTER EIGHT

Just Enough

So then, just as you received Christ Jesus as Lord, continue to live in Him...

Colossians 2:6

With the hustle and bustle of the Bay Area in my rearview mirror, in January 1985 I guided my Toyota Celica north up I-5 to Oregon. Carefree and optimistic, I looked forward to seeing what lay ahead.

By summer of that year, Dad and I had found our way back to the golf course on a regular basis. In his fifties by then, my dad still played good golf, shooting a 65 for eighteen holes—two shots off the course record. One evening when the two of us played, I walked off the fourth tee to ask Dad, "How'd you hit that drive?"

"I hit it well," he replied. Moments later, we came to a ball 225 yards (or so) down the fairway; I paused to point to my ball about ten yards ahead of his. I said, "Dad, your golf ball is here, and you're away." He smiled, hit his shot and then, walking up to my shot, said, "Son, I'm glad I was wrong all those years ago. You're hitting the ball right out with me. I'm proud of you and all you've achieved."

But back in January, it didn't take long to realize that I'd exchanged the monotony of daily commutes for other realities. With my stepsisters gone, the home was less chaotic; however, given my immaturity and my stepmom's nature, our relationship remained contentious at times. Winter was cold and wet. And most of all, I felt the pressure of a clock that ticked. I needed to find a job.

Within weeks I was hired as Media Director at a small Albany branch office of a Portland advertising agency. I moved into an apartment of my own, but with only a couple of acquaintances in town from my high school days, solo trips to the store, theatre, library or new mall quickly grew old. By April, I was bored stiff again, my heart wanting something more.

Alone one Saturday night, I briefly entertained the thought of going to a nightclub. But instead, God let me recall "just enough" of my church experience in San Francisco that my fingers walked a Yellow Pages phone book straight to the heading of "Churches."

Just Enough

Northwest Hills Church was located about ten miles from Albany—in Corvallis, home to Oregon State University (OSU). A graduate of Oregon, I didn't care for OSU (a rival in sports). But I liked the students I met that Sunday at the church. Several of them encouraged me to come back to the church that night for a rehearsal of an upcoming college-and-career-age singles musical "Psalms Alive." I couldn't read a note or carry a tune, but it didn't matter. Over the next eight weeks I had a blast with fifty new friends, and by the performance had acquired the art of lip-syncing to choruses of passages from the biblical book.

My decision to go to church proved a good step. I didn't realize at the time that "just enough" was a pattern for how I approached life.

Once I'd tried something—acquired "just enough" knowledge or experience to enjoy some success—I'd feel ready to tackle something else. With "just enough" confidence in a skill, or a "gut" feel as to what seemed logical, I'd take a next step. I'd tick one goal off the list to head to the next.

I'd known "just enough" to go to church rather than to slip into a bar for a night. Through most of my twenties, over a period of five years that were pivotal to my spiritual growth, God kept me moving forward in faith by showing me "just enough" of what I needed next. I didn't look to cut corners ("just enough"); I just followed God as He led.

September 1985, the year I returned, Phil, a college-and-career-age pastor, encouraged those of his "flock" to get involved in small-group Bible study. Kevin, a friend and study leader I'd gotten to know, invited me to attend his group. A study struck me as "just enough" of the next best thing to do, so I signed up and went.

My first night there, I wondered if I'd made the right move. Kevin asked us to identify fifty things we observed in the first four verses of the biblical book of 1 John. Silently, I sat incredulous as others proved it could be done. Impressed as I was by it, I wasn't moved to read the Bible that year; however, the group had plenty to keep me coming back—the girls were cute! Some weeks Kevin asked me to meet him for ice cream. Our talks most times turned comfortably spiritual, supplying me "just enough" to stir my heart more in my faith.

In the spring of 1986, Kevin rocked me from my complacency. "Greg," he said, "Pastor Phil would like to meet with you." *Uh-oh, they're on to me. This gig is up.* I slumped into a chair beside Pastor Phil's desk. "Kevin and I have been talking," Phil said, "and we think you should consider leading a study group of your own this summer." *You've got the wrong guy here, Bub.* But my church and study experience had taught me "just enough" to tell Phil: "I'll pray about it."

I went home, and I prayed—best as I knew how. A few days later, I felt "just enough" of some perceived prompting within me to go back to Phil and say, "Okay. I'll give this a try."

Weeks later, scared spitless, I studied six verses of Psalm 1 like I'd never studied the Bible before (I hadn't!). I bought a study Bible, read commentaries (insights of theologians) and asked questions of about every Christian I knew. I also prayed—a lot! Trembling, I opened our group by saying, "I don't know what I'm doing. I'll need your help." God blessed my honesty, and our meetings went well. In August, Phil asked if I would lead a group for the upcoming school year. This time I knew "more than enough." Enthusiastically, I said, "Yes."

I facilitated study groups for the next three years. I especially enjoyed Monday evenings, when about a dozen group leaders would gather at Pastor Phil's home. We'd dine with Phil and his family. Then, after dinner we'd move to the living room, where Phil would mentor us in the biblical passage that we'd teach to our groups later that week. Between Phil's knowledge and my increased preparation, I started to hunger more for the truths of God's Word.

Born Wrong, Made Right

I embraced Pastor Phil as a spiritual guide, but I also respected him for another reason. Sometimes in mid-conversation, Phil's lips would move, but no words would come out. Moments later, he'd typically pop back to pick up about where he'd left off. For decades, Phil suffered from temporal lobe epilepsy. By the mid-1990s, his condition had worsened. A series of grand-mal seizures required several surgeries. Through these surgeries, and God's healing touch, Phil's seizures are mostly controlled and have not been a major problem since.

I perceived that Phil's health concerns were more trying for him to deal with than anything I'd faced. Phil needed medication and invasive medical procedures that my deformities never required. My thoughts may have been inaccurate, but the two of us agreed about this: What people see and perceive of defects—epilepsy, amputations, deformities or whatever—isn't necessarily a person's greatest challenge. Physically *made right*, according to the Designer's intent, people's souls are "disabled," *born wrong* in sin. Romans 3:23 says, "For all have sinned and fall short of the glory of God." Jesus died to take care of this.

Born Right

In Eugene one night in the mid-1980s, I joined friends for a concert by singer-songwriter Michael W. Smith. In the middle of his concert, Smith stopped to recite from memory all of Psalm 139. My heart was captivated by a few of its lines:

> "For You created my inmost being; You knit me together in my mother's womb. I praise You because I am fearfully and wonderfully made; Your works are wonderful, I know that full well. My frame was not hidden from You when I was made in the secret place, when I was woven together in the depths of the earth. Your eyes saw my unformed body; all the days ordained for me were written in Your book before one of them came to be" (verses 13-16).

Smith spoke to hundreds of fans that night; however, I felt as if God, through the singer, spoke personally to me. The next morning, and for weeks after that, I raced to Psalm 139 to reflect on the verses that affirmed God's unconditional love and acceptance of me. God was not absent, disconnected or distant when I was made—"His eyes saw my unformed body." Wow! *I had, after all, been made right!* I didn't yet get that I didn't need to prove it.

It's not easy to think it's true that every child arrives *born right*. Seeing conjoined twins, babies with Down syndrome, autism or other defects is troubling. These cases are tough. A newborn died in the arms of a couple I know, hours after the baby's birth, due to an abnormality. Brutally painful as that was, they came to accept that God, sovereign, hadn't made a mistake. Now, each year on the anniversary of their child's birth, they shed tears of sorrow and grief, also giving thanks to God for His gift. God grew their hearts through the experience. Feeling hand-picked for this adversity, they come alongside parents in similar situations of need with comfort they are uniquely equipped to provide.

I've spoken with what, I admit, is a very small sampling of parents of children of special needs. None of their journeys have been easy, but in each case they've adjusted. Sometimes it's taken them years to reach a point of acceptance, but these parents have come to love and accept the child (or children) that God has given them.

God authors no junk. He makes no mistakes. Heavy, tall, "broken," pimply or small, Psalm 139 affirms God as a magnificent Creator. Leila of the church who visited me at birth was right. Nothing is shocking to God, our Maker.

Evidence of Growth

During those years, my gazes in the mirror began to reflect a person I liked better. Although I'd always projected self-confidence, I'd often felt insecure. Friendships, my leadership of groups and a steadier diet of God's Word helped bolster my esteem.

By 1987, I'd made a couple of moves and found my way into "The White House." It was a large two-story white house located two blocks from the OSU campus that guys from the church had rotated in and out of for years. Unwittingly, housemates groomed me in some life lessons. Through their example, I became more relational, learning how to take criticism (and, no doubt, dish it out). Best of all, I found joy in participating in good, clean fun.

We snow-sledded down hills on kitchen cutting boards, hosted non-alcoholic dances, and pranked one another, and others, continually. I still chuckle when I think about Eric standing beside our dinner table, muttering, "Guys. I think I have a problem; my urine's blue." Rich, a chemist in the home, had spiked Eric's orange juice that morning with methylene blue. (Eric was fine.) In January, we'd make it to the coast for "polar-bear swims" in the icy surf of the Pacific. Summers, we'd raft Class IV rapids down the Deschutes River—everything we did building a lifetime of memories.

Greater social skills and Bible knowledge—God's Word becoming more of a road map for my life—compelled me to take relationship risks.

One day I decided it was time to go deep. First I spoke with Mom, and then later with Dad. I wanted to hear their thoughts as to why they'd split. My folks talked openly with me about things they felt had contributed to a failed marriage. Once, I'd prayed to God to acknowledge things I'd done, and words I'd said, as a teen that I knew had hurt my parents and stepparents. I'd felt the forgiveness of God (1 John 1:9); however, I now felt the Spirit of God (Jesus alive within me) compel me to go to all four of them, a set at a time,

Mom (my hero) and my stepdad

and ask forgiveness for what I'd done. I wanted to ensure that I would no longer have reason to feel angry or bitter.

"Would you please forgive me for ...?" I read from my list, uncertain as to how they'd respond.

"Yes," they replied. "Please forgive us, too." Tears flowed with hugs all around, in what marked a fresh start into relationships much more loving and kind with my parents and stepparents, too.

Maturing some, I also started to fare a little better with women. At age twenty-five, I had my first "girlfriend"—about six months of sweet dates with a gal six years younger than me whom I liked. But when she went to college and met a guy, I drifted back to being that "one-date wonder."

One day I went on an outing to the Oregon Coast with a girl I'd known for years. I got a little twitch and voiced a tinge of my warm feelings. She said those words I'd heard before: "I just want to be friends." Then, on our drive home, she told me how she'd made a vow to God to only "court" Him for an entire year. Intrigued, I heard her out, and then I decided I'd give it a shot.

For twelve months, and then for another year, I "dated" only God.

I looked to cultivate a more intimate relationship with God, and with my Savior, Jesus. We spent lots of time with one another, sometimes whole days together as I'd talk with Him or try to quiet myself to listen in prayer. In response to God's Word that I often read, I'd find creative ways to "Love the Lord your God with all your heart and with all your soul and with all your mind" (Matthew 22:37).

We'd hang in the arboretum, and amble beside Oregon's pristine mountain streams. I'd sit atop ocean bluffs to feel His presence and pleasure, as I'd breathe the mist of the salt air or drink in the seaside's beauty. I encountered my God as I'd never imagined possible, the two of us growing closer.

Books I read schooled me on important topics. A.W. Tozer's *The Pursuit of God*, Alan L. McGinnis' *The Friendship Factor* and Dick Purnell's *Becoming a Friend and Lover* became like best friends to me. They provided me with needed perspective. Through my decision not to date, I became good friends with some women. They became more than "objects" I needed for a relationship, or in the hopes to someday be married. By age twenty-eight, I felt convinced of this: *God, should You choose, I can live content with You and no one else.*

That Student's Note

By 1987, at twenty-six years of age, I'd earned my teaching credentials.

I had done my student teaching at West Albany High School. One quarter I shadowed Jim, an excellent instructor and a Vietnam vet who had lost an arm in the war. One day, as I struggled again to fasten that top button of my dress shirt, I asked Jim for help. He fumbled a bit and then blurted out, "How about this? Seven fingers between us, and we still can't get the job done." We shared a hearty laugh. Sometimes it's good to chuckle and laugh—especially at ourselves. I've laughed when a couple of friends have joked about "shaking my finger." Or when I give a high-five (a two-and-a-half) and let a friend know that "I'll keep the change." Or when I eat with chopsticks and another person can't, I like to jest that they're over-qualified—too many fingers, perhaps.

After student-teaching, I found a permanent position at South Albany High School, my alma mater. Some days I taught students English. Other days, my students taught me. Remember that letter with my name in ALL CAPS? Here it is again—this time, in full, just as I received it.

```
        I REALLY DON'T KNOW HOW TO START THIS SO I'LL COME RIGHT TO THE POINT.
THE FIRST TIME I WALKED INTO YOU CLASSROOM I NOTICED SOMETHING AS A MATTER
OF FACT I THINK THE WHOLE CLASS DID. YOU ARE PROBABLY WONDERING WHAT THIS
NOTE IS ALL ABOUT,OR YOU PROBABLY ALREADY DO,YES MR.STOUGHTON IT IS YOUR—
HANDS. DO YOU REALLT THINK YOUR BEING FAIR TO US,BY NOT TELLING US WHAT H-
APPENED? YOU EXPECT US TO DO GOOD IN YOUR CLASS;FACE THE FRONT,AND PAY AT-
TETION,HOW CAN WE DO THAT WHN YOUR IN THE FRONT OF THE ROOM WAVING YOUR H-
ANDS AROUND LIKE NOTHING IS WRONG WITH THEM. WRONG MR. STOUGHTON SOMETHING
IS WRONG WITH THEM,AND I THINK IT IS VERY UNFAIR OF YOU TO KEEP THAT FROM,
US. WE HAVE WRITTEN DOWN THINGS ABOUT OURSELVES,UOR FAMILYS,AND WHAT WE D-
ID OVER THE WEEKEND,WHAT HAVE YOU TOLD US ABOUT YOURSELF,WELL LETS JUST SAY THIS,
'N O T   E N O U G H'
        SO MR. STOUGHTON AFTER YOU HAVE READ THIS I HOPE YOU REALIZE WHAT KIND OF
SITUATION YOU ARE PUTTING US IN,"A VERY AWKWARD ONE"
OH,AND I DON'T MEAN TO HURT YOUR FEELINGS OR BRING BACK ANY PAINFUL MEMORIES,
BUT LIKE THEY SAY ON T.V. "E N Q U I R I N G   M I N D S   W A N T   T O   K N O W"
SO MAYBE YOU SHOULD TAKE A LITTLE TIME OUT OF YOUR BUSY SCHEDUAL,AND TELL US
WHAT HAPPENED,AND LET US ASK SOME QUESTIONS,WERE ONLY KIDS,AND MOST KIDS ARE
ABOUT THINGS,SUCH AS YOUR HANDS BUT ARE AFRAID TO ASK.
MR. STOUGHTON I REALLY HOPE YOU DECIDE TO TELL US THE TRUTH,
DON'T YOU THINK YOU OWE US THAT?



                SINCERLY,
                    A CURIOUS KID
```

My first thought: *Why should I? My hands, they're such a small thing.*

In part, I hadn't told them about my hands because I didn't give my deformities any thought. It had been a long time since Mrs.

Kenneth's first-grade class and those days when John wanted to beat me up.

I also wondered: *What would I share? What would I say? "Inquiring minds WANT to know." Really? Are others that curious?* By the end of the day, I'd decided that teaching topic sentences could wait. The next day I'd share with each class what had happened.

Early that evening, I replayed events from my childhood. I thought about the words of that doctor and my parent's choice to shower me with their love. Then my mind went to what I'd achieved. I'd slayed the pegboard and climbed the rope. I'd come to play the drums, ride a unicycle, make free throws, and play golf reasonably well.

Then, it felt like a switch turned on in my head. *There's more to my story than that. They should know that life is sometimes messy and hard.* I'd tell them about my broken home, my need to move, and how I walked the halls of their campus downcast. *I know more of them can relate to that.*

The light grew brighter. *I can't leave them there.* In a public school, I didn't need to "preach," but they'd need to know there's more to my story. They'd hear that because of God, I'm "fearfully and wonderfully made." I'd remind them that peer pressure isn't smart and how alcohol had nearly tanked me. But that wasn't the end of my story. I'd found God and entered into a personal relationship with Jesus to experience forgiveness. I'd changed and found a way to walk these halls with a peace and joy that my life once lacked.

All this was true. Jesus was making a difference in my life. And God was priming the pump for me to deal with a little bit more.

Repeatedly, my mind kept going back over one line that night, and it disturbed me. "MAYBE YOU SHOULD TAKE A LITTLE TIME OUT OF YOUR BUSY SCHEDULE AND TELL US WHAT HAPPENED." The girl who came forward the next day to tell me she'd typed the note was right. I'd been nailed to the wall by a ninth grader. In wanting to make a good first impression, I'd failed to be emotionally present with the students I was trying so hard to impact.

The next day, I sat perched on a stool, my shoes and socks off, letting down my guard to tell them about my life. I even apologized to them for my busyness and neglect—which this student had mentioned. My classes rewarded me with some kind words and three days of good behavior. It proved to be a home run. That girl helped more than she'll likely ever know.

For the first time, I'd publicly shared my story. It felt good and right to do it. I liked how God had let me be an inspiration, seeing I had a story of His love and goodness to tell. I hadn't realized that through my process of preparation, God had opened the lid to a can inside my heart.

Within months, that can had a label.

Perfectionism and God's Grace

As a first-year English teacher, I made another rookie mistake. I chose to coach freshman boys' basketball. Between prepping for classes and practices, reading essays, and traveling to away games, I averaged about five hours of sleep a night over several months. By spring, and the end of a long and so-so season (ten wins, seventeen losses), I was exhausted.

One night, thinking I might catch up on my sleep, I stayed closer to school at my parents' house. About midnight, overcome with anxiety and emotion, I slumped to the kitchen floor. Hearing my cry, Dad left his bedroom and walked down the hall to be at my side. "Greg, what's wrong?" he asked.

"Dad, I taught really well today," I said. "But I'm afraid. I don't know that I can teach as well tomorrow. I'm anxious and depressed, and I think I need some counsel." Dad agreed, and so did God, my heavenly Father.

"You've got a bad case of perfectionism," diagnosed a counselor by the end of our first meeting. In time, he told me he felt I had tried to compensate for my deformities. "You were born right," he said, "and you've set out to prove it. You've got a crisis of identity." With my parents' breakup and then sports ripped away, I'd turned toward achievements to earn praise and prove my worth. All along, I'd been building my identity on a shaky foundation—performance.

"Have you heard of God's grace?" he asked. I said I had and referred back to Pastor Ken's teaching. "You're a child of God, loved and accepted by Him," he said. "To Him you are, like every person, someone of infinite worth." He went on to define grace as "God's unmerited favor." He further explained how God's rescue of me hadn't come as a result of the work of my hands. He'd worked on my behalf, sending His Son, Jesus. "That's how deeply He loves you," he said.

He added: "I believe you fear failure because of what happens when you achieve. You get 'strokes' from others. When you can rest in God's affirmation of you, you have nothing to prove. You'll feel less like you have to be perfect. Ironically, that'll take some work."

Practically, he asked if I might look to God to retool my thinking. He encouraged me to repeat three phrases aloud, or silently, to myself as many times as I could each day: 1) *I'm wonderfully loved and accepted by God*; 2) *In Christ, I'm completely and totally forgiven*; and 3) *I don't have to be perfect, but very good is good enough*. As a visual cue, he asked me to turn a desk askew before each class, against my normal preference for neat and tidy rows. Mostly, it worked—at least at that time.

From San Francisco, at twenty-three years of age, I'd come "home" to Oregon—an anticipated return to the known, comfortable and familiar. God had a different plan. God took me to Oregon for a season of massive growth. Bible studies, roommates, dates—and what would be a brief teaching experience—all led to a better understanding of myself through the lens of God, my Maker.

Unbeknownst to me, God had also used this time to prep me "just enough" to take another leap of faith.

A few months before my twenty-ninth birthday, I was about to venture out again—this time beyond any place I'd ever been. A twelve-foot U-Haul with a car in tow was packed in front of my home. Another friend (named Phil) and I were ready to travel east.

Rethink It

1. Write or share any ways you think or feel you might have been *born wrong*?

Think Differently to Unleash Your Potential

2. Turn to page 84 and Psalm 139:13-16. Reread the verses several times. Do you believe what God says about you in this passage is true? Why or why not?

3. Rethink your list of limitations. (This was your answer to the first question in chapter 1's "Rethink It" section.)

Write a verse or the verses of Psalm 139:13-16. Make copies and then tape them in places where you'll see them throughout your day (mirror, refrigerator, desktop at work). Read and give thought to what God says is true about you.

Pick a physical feature or personality trait that concerns you. Say a brief sentence prayer: "I thank you, God, for _____ (name of limiting trait)." God wants you to think differently about yourself!

What else may be limiting you?

4. Are there ways in which you're living overly "performance-based"? How is your identity (worth and significance) tied to your achievements, accolades or "perfectionistic" tendencies?

5. Grace is defined as receiving something we didn't earn and don't deserve. What are your thoughts about forgiveness and the topic of God's grace?

6. If you give thought to your spouse, children, added family and friends, are there ways you relate that you need to rethink? How better can you show grace to others?

To experience more of God's grace, look up and read the following verses found in the Bible: Jeremiah 31:3, Psalm 103:12, Ephesians 2:8-9, 2 Corinthians 12:9.

To think differently about God's grace and how it applies personally to you, spend time reading and meditating on the recommended verses above. Take a moment to thank God for the grace He has made available to you to help you unleash your potential.

CHAPTER NINE

Heading East—and Beyond

Adventure is worthwhile in itself.

Amelia Earhart

After a five-day, cross-country trek in a truck and trailer with my car in tow, Phil and I arrived in Cincinnati, Ohio, on February 20, 1990. A harrowing four-hour, fifty-mile crawl in a white-out across the Rocky Mountains and the Continental Divide made Cincinnati, with its unseasonably blue skies, a more pleasant sight than I'd expected. Nestled against its seven hills, the city made a striking first impression. It was easy to see why, as far back as 1820, many of its proud citizens had called Cincinnati the "Queen City" or "Queen of the West."

Not quite love at first sight, whatever fondness I had for the city was put to the test. Though hungry for adventure, my heart nearly met its match during my first week in Cincinnati.

First, nature unleashed its fury. Eight inches of heavy, wet snow fell, followed by an extreme drop in temperature. It was nowhere near as cold as when, while I was in Oregon, I watched the NFL's Cincinnati Bengals host the coldest football game in the league's history, on a day of minus-fifty-two-degree wind chill. However, my body temperature fell when, on my second day there, the engine of my car went kaput on a suburban street. Things got worse. The following day I got a case of the stomach flu. For two full days, I lay flat on my back in the home of a colleague I'd just met. I regained strength to sign a lease on an apartment in Mason, Ohio, an hour before the U-Haul had to be returned. My furniture and boxes unloaded, Phil said, "Good-bye and good luck. I'll be praying for you," and caught his ride to Indiana as planned. I fell to the couch and buried my head beneath a comforter. I had no transportation and was living in a place with no lights, refrigeration or heat for my first twenty-four hours.

Rather ironically, I'd interviewed with a representative of Procter and Gamble my senior year at Oregon. Presuming I'd go into advertising, I hadn't bothered to take time to research the company. So I didn't know the marketing giant's headquarters were in Cincinnati. My session "rocked" until the interviewer asked, "How do you feel about relocating to Ohio?"

"Ugh, I don't see myself living there—ever," I replied. That ended that! Now, years later, here I was in Cincinnati—this seemingly horrific place.

I Surrender

About a year before making the long-distance move, I'd attended a regional gathering of mostly college students in a hotel in Portland, hosted by Campus Crusade for Christ (CCC—now Cru in the United States). There, its founder and president, the late Dr. Bill Bright, challenged us to "Come help change the world." He explained how we could use our gifts to help others receive the same message of Christ we'd each received. My interest was piqued, and I walked across a hallway to join a smaller group of about one hundred people who also wanted to hear more.

The prior year, Steve, one of my roommates in The White House, invited me to some CCC campus gatherings, studies and events. I'd found it a good fit. At the conference, though, my jaw dropped when Steve took the mic and talked of his recent decision to join the ministry. News to me—my heart skipped and my mind raced. *God, this is wild! Is this a step of faith that You are asking me to take, too?* During an invite to pray, I sensed a whisper of God I'd learned to hear—Him wooing me to respond. *Okay, God. I'm all in—whatever it means, whatever it takes.*

By the spring of that year, I'd committed to CCC, resigned from teaching, and stressed my parents. (The organization required me to raise funds for my salary.) In the summer I car-pooled with a guy to Colorado State University to take some Bible classes and, while there, figure out exactly what I might do for work. My passion for sports and God intersected in an opportunity offered by the ministry's sports division, Athletes in Action (AIA). With them, I'd have opportunity to use my advertising, journalism and coaching experience.

I only saw one problem: The AIA office was located in Cincinnati.

Disheartened, I climbed atop my bed in a dormitory room at CSU, opened an atlas to the USA map, and prayed. A couple of hours later, I'd surrendered to what I sensed God desired. *Yes, Lord, I'll do it.* It was the first of a few times since that I've wrestled with God over geography. He's always won, and I'm glad. It's worked out well.

Eight months later, my chilled body buried beneath a comforter, I screamed and shook my fist at God—in prayer, of course: *Lord, what have You done?*

I reasoned that things could only get better. They did. The next morning the power came on. The next week, I got my car back from the mechanic and started my job. The following month, I sat in a chair on the court after an NBA game to interview Cleveland Cavalier guard, Mark Price, in person. Seated face to face with a professional basketball great, I thought I'd died and gone to heaven.

The Power of Focus

By June of 1990, I'd settled in Cincinnati and transitioned well. Yet, eager to escape from the summer heat, I jumped at the chance to travel to Colorado. My boss, Lillie, had invited me to take part in an AIA "spiritual training camp" for collegiate athletes. I'd go through the camp to be better equipped to write about it—a participatory journalism sort of week.

No one told me about "The Special."

At about 7 a.m. on a Saturday morning, camp leaders herded us into cars for an hour-long ride into the Rocky Mountains. Our car stopped, and I heard, "We're here." At once I sniffed trouble. A rather gaunt-looking gent trotted in front of us wearing short-shorts, a tank top and a number pinned to his back. Moments later we were told that we'd "compete" in an eight-mile mountain run followed by a nineteen-mile bike ride once back in town. *How special.*

The gun sounded. Mile one was a blast. Mile two proved a little more difficult. By mile three, I wondered if God had sucked all the oxygen from Colorado. Near the peak, I walked slowly—encouraged, though, by passing a few football linemen who crawled on their hands and knees. I reached the summit. My body writhed in pain. I wanted to quit, yet I knew I couldn't—with no way home but down the mountain.

The prior night a camp leader had concluded his Bible lesson with a group activity. He instructed each of us to take two popsicle sticks from a bag, break one and glue it to the other to form a small cross. With a permanent marker, he asked us to write on the small wooden object a Scripture reference that would be of spiritual inspiration and help. Mine read: Hebrews 12:1-3.

On the summit, drained of energy, I reached my left hand into the waistband of my shorts and took hold of this cross. I lifted it in front of my chest and fixed my gaze on it. I thought of that passage of Scripture—verses I'd committed to memory that week:

"Therefore, since we are surrounded by such a great cloud of witnesses, let us throw off everything that hinders and the sin that so easily entangles, and let us run with perseverance the race marked out for us. Let us fix our eyes on Jesus, the author and perfecter of our faith, who for the joy set before Him endured the cross, scorning its shame, and sat down at the right hand of the throne of God. Consider Him who endured such opposition from sinful men, so that you will not grow weary and lose heart" (Hebrews 12:1-3).

My focus shifted. As I turned my thoughts toward Jesus and contemplated the torture He'd endured during His arrest and crucifixion, my pain subsided. In comparison to Christ, I'd never know what it is to suffer. I caught my second wind.

As if riding on the wings of eagles, I sprinted downhill with ease and crossed the finish line. I took a few deep breaths. Then, be it runner's high or an actual moment of selflessness, I turned and ran a quarter of a mile back up the hill. There were others (mostly football linemen) who hadn't finished the race, and I wanted to provide some encouragement. Soon I crossed the line to finish a second time.

Two hours later, back in Fort Collins, my finger and half-thumb pinched the cross to the handlebars of a bike. I pedaled nineteen miles through the city's trails and streets, my focus on God powerfully supplying the perspective and strength I needed to persevere.

In the almost three decades since, I've faced countless times of challenge. My faith doesn't inoculate me from life's problems or tests; however, it gives me One to whom I can turn. In a relationship *with* Jesus, oftentimes, God shrinks my mountains to molehills. My work is to trust Him by faith and pray—His power at work within me to focus and persevere.

Love and Marriage

I returned from Colorado to think that—God willing—I would trust Him for a spouse. For twenty-four months, I'd encountered God in richly satisfying ways. We'd grown close, but the hopes I'd had that I might one day marry hadn't gone away. Yet, again, I'd really come to believe that Jesus was all I'd need. Single or married, I could make it, mostly content. Feeling free of some of the pressure I'd formerly felt, I returned to Cincinnati ready to date.

My third Sunday in Ohio, I'd met Linda DeYoung at West Chester Church. An attractive brunette with beautiful big blue eyes and a pretty smile, she immediately caught my eye. Over the next few months, we became friends through career-age group socials and a Bible study I led. I liked her looks, and I liked her personality. Linda, more introverted than me, was soft-spoken, gentle and kind. Sold on the thought that opposites attract, in July 1990 I picked up the phone and asked her out.

On our first date, we had pizza and drove to a Cincinnati Reds baseball game. I figured we were God's perfect match when an elderly ticket-taker traded us (the cute young couple) our tickets for his two—some lower-level seats. We had a great evening, and I sensed a green light to date again.

By our third outing, I was utterly smitten. Linda's loveliness sparkled against the backdrop of Buckeye Falls at Sharon Woods Park. I barely noticed the scenery, though, as I fumbled to tell her of the love I already felt in my heart. For Linda, that was a bit too early and a bit too much. She asked that I give her some space. I did. A few weeks later, she agreed to dinner at my place. I cooked, we ate and then I cued up the movie *The Man from Snowy River*. By then her emotions had caught up. We agreed to be a couple. A year later, I proposed and Linda said yes. Ten months later, on June 27, 1992—with Mike, my Oregon friend, roommate and spiritual guide at my side as best man—Linda and I were wed in Cincinnati.

Lobster-Claw Syndrome (Ectrodactyly)

Months into our courtship, but before we were engaged, Linda and I talked about my deformities. I shared with her what I knew about my hands and feet, and how it could affect us if we were to marry and ever have children. With reasonable confidence, I told her it was a fifty-fifty chance that a child of mine could be born similarly deformed. To Linda, it was of no concern, and we never talked about it again.

A few years earlier, Dad had paid for me to get a day of genetic counseling at Oregon Health and Science University in Portland. There, a team of specialists conducted a thorough examination. They reviewed the issues of my mom's pregnancy, the birth itself, sets of

X-rays past and present, and records of my surgeries. They poked and prodded my hands and feet and then took a deep dive into their thick medical books. They concluded that my condition was ectrodactyly, or split-hand/split-foot malformation, also referred to as "lobster claw syndrome."

In short, and in lay terms, ectrodactyly is a rare genetic birth disorder that affects about one of every ninety thousand babies born. One of thousands of genes that make up our twenty-three pairs of chromosomes is slightly altered and then paired so as to cause an "abortion" of one or more of the middle digits of the hands and/or feet. Though it's a genetic disorder, it's not always present in the parents of a newborn, as is true in my case.

I can count on my few fingers those I've heard about or met who have hands like mine. As a boy, I watched a TV special on Bree Walker, a woman with limbs like mine who once anchored the San Diego news.

Then in my forties, Dad wrote a "Letter to the Editor" that ran in the March 2005 issue of *Golf Digest*.

In his letter, Dad shared how my deformities hadn't limited my ability to play golf. Weeks later, Dad received a letter from the father of a five-year-old boy in Nevada whose hands resembled mine. On separate calls, Dad and I encouraged this boy's father. In Orlando, my home since 2008, I've met two people with my condition. One is a local pastor. The other is a beautiful young girl who, through the unconditional love of wonderful and godly parents, is thriving. By first grade, she was winning age-level swim events.

Marriage and Greater Grace

In more than twenty-five years of marriage, Linda has unconditionally embraced my physical differences. Now, as to my insides, she's accepted those, too—at times with a little more challenge.

As is true of many honeymoons, ours ended too quickly. A year into our marriage, we grew tense and impatient; our communication became strained. The dysfunction I'd known at home indicated that married people should expect to verbally argue and fight. Conversely, Linda's family isn't one to show emotion. In our marital spats, I wanted to "hammer things out"—right NOW—and get closure. Often Linda fled, wanting space. Typical Psychology 101: fight or flight. We just didn't know it.

Humorous in retrospect, but not at all at the time, I once chased Linda from one room to another throughout our small home. She'd slam doors behind her. Unable to

---

Profiles in courage

December: *Don't Believe His Handicap, by Dave Kindred*

The excellent story on David Gaudin brought back memories from 1961. Our son, Greg, was born with congenital deformities: no middle finger and a deformed thumb on the left hand, only a thumb and middle finger on his right hand, and a similar configuration on his feet. I was an assistant pro at that time, a previous three-sport athlete, and devastated.

Similar to Gaudin's doctors' words to his parents—"Nature makes mistakes. Take the ball and go with it"—our doctor, a kindly orthopedist, advised, "If you want a freak, hide him in the closet, and that's what you will have. If you want a normal boy, treat him as one."

We tried to heed that advice, and are proud to say that Greg has achieved beyond our greatest expectations. Though his time on the golf course has been more limited than he would like, he plays to about a 12-handicap, and since he was 16, I have never been able to beat him at H-O-R-S-E.
Bob Stoughton, Albany, Ore.

flee my verbal tantrum, Linda raced out the front door to climb into the cab of our Toyota pickup truck on a bitterly cold winter night. And she locked the doors! *Who does something like that?*

It seemed a good time for professional help.

Both of us strong in Christ, we've always been committed to and trusting of one another. Our marriage was never in trouble, but we both needed to adjust and grow up. For me, my perfectionistic tendencies once more slithered in, this time impacting our relationship. Prone to hold myself to standards I couldn't attain, I, too, had unrealistic expectations. I'd married a terrific woman, and in that first year, I'd asked her to be God's "superwoman" on steroids. The counselor said, "Let's work some on grace." Asking God to help me be more accepting and less critical, I made some progress. We both learned a few communication techniques for how to "fight fair" verbally.

About five years later, in yet another context, a similar problem arose. I was in a peer review with a Human Resources person with AIA, who said, "Greg, you do many things well, but I have a concern." *Oh, what's that?* "I want to strongly encourage you to learn more about how to apply God's grace to your life. Otherwise I think your life and leadership might suffer." I learned about how I'd unwittingly put a young gal "under the pile" in a performance review I'd done by rattling off a list of things she could improve. *If she failed, I failed, and I didn't want that to happen.*

Driven to get better (of course), I checked out a pile of Christian books with "grace" in the title. Writers illustrated stories of people whose lives had come to exemplify greater grace. I found God not to be the "taskmaster" I'd made Him out to be. I saw that God wanted me to work *with* Him, more than *for* Him—a distinction I hadn't yet understood. Also, I saw that *who I am* to Him matters more than *what I do*. I also began paying more attention to certain Bible verses on the topic. This one was of particular help then: "My grace is sufficient for you, for my power is made perfect in weakness. Therefore, I will boast all the more gladly about my weaknesses, so that Christ's power may rest on me" (2 Corinthians 12:9).

Twenty years later, I've gotten better—this by the grace of God. Most days now (unless I'm writing about my perfectionistic tendencies), my walk in Jesus is one of greater grace.

Two Great Blessings

January 16, 1996, our love reached new heights when we celebrated the birth of our first son, Kyle. As Linda recovered from twenty hours of labor and a C-section delivery, I cradled our boy in my arms. I looked to our son's fingers and toes, counting each of them to see a baby who was complete in that way. We'd taken a leap of faith. With a fifty-fifty chance that Kyle could be born with defects, God had allowed the coin to land on "heads."

Two years later, we thought it was time to have a second child. Five years and a few infertility tests later, it still hadn't happened. Linda had been praying, and she thought we should adopt a child. At age forty and able to do the math, I told her I thought that she'd gone mad. Then one night we babysat Dani, our friends' cute little two-year-old daughter, who was adopted from India. As I lay on the couch that night, Dani hoisted herself up on my lap to giggle, laugh and play. *Alright, Lord, I'll do it!* God had answered Linda's prayers.

On March 4, 2003, God showed us a beautiful parallel that exists between an adoption of a child and His adoption of us spiritually in a relationship with Jesus. At the Detroit Airport, a Korean businessman exited customs to hand Linda a beautiful six-month-old boy—our second son, Soo Bin Ko. He reached up with his hands to caress Linda's face.

In America, it seemed *wrong* to have a boy named "Sue." We named our son Ryan Ko Stoughton. Both of our sons are unique and are equally, unconditionally loved and embraced,  ranking high on a list of our greatest blessings.

Only God Does This!

It's been almost thirty years since I made the move to Cincinnati. Over that span, life has had its twists, turns, peaks and valleys on a ride of many surprises. To recall a sampling of happenings is to reflect on what I regard as a life of adventure, fulfillment and blessing.

Many times I've looked back to think: *Only God does something like this!*

I've had the opportunity to be around many sports personalities. Los Angeles baseball manager Joe Torre tipped me $400 after three days of fun when I cleaned cleats in the Dodger locker room during some MLB exhibition games. Then there was the time I picked up the phone to hear the voice of former Washington Redskins coach and NASCAR team owner Joe Gibbs: "Thank you, Greg, for your work on

Los Angeles Dodger Manager Joe Torre

my brochure and the writing of the booklet (*Fourth and One—a Bible Study for Men*)." Moments like these are insignificant in life's larger picture, but they've made for some fun memories—some experiences where I scratch my head and think: *Only God does this!*

One night I blew an opportunity. About forty-five minutes before an AIA basketball game at UCLA, I turned around in Pauley Pavilion to see legendary UCLA basketball coach John Wooden take his seat—the two of us mostly alone. Nervous, I froze. I shook his hand with my lips struggling to move: "Uh, Coach, nice to meet you. Um, I love your book." *God, I'd take a mulligan on that!*

The things God does shouldn't be of surprise. He is God, and I am not. Yet, often His work exceeds my expectations.

In 2001, God led a few of us to launch what's become the nation's largest local chapter of Upward Basketball–Upward Sports, a national program for youth. Today, fifteen hundred kids participate annually in a collaborative effort of ten churches in the suburb of West Chester, Ohio. Thousands of people have learned about Christ, with kids receiving instruction about Him and life-changing principles. *Only God does this!*

Then, in God's goodness, He does things like this! He plucks a boy from the backwoods of Toledo, Oregon, and sends him to more than thirty countries to help impact lives. There are a few photos on the wall of my home office I cherish:

- There's a picture taken in the hot, Zimbabwean sun where I'm sketching a diagram of the significance of the cross, and God's rescue of us in Jesus, to three African teens (Charles, Benjamin and Paxson).

- Another photo reminds me to pray, be generous and serve. I'm pouring soup into the bowl of a young girl, incredibly hungry, whose "home" was a tin shed outside Cape Town, South Africa. I got to go home and fill my belly. The next day, she was hungry again.

- And then there's the picture that reminds me of the week I spent with a church group in a Haitian village in the Dominican Republic. In 105-degree heat, we worked with locals to construct a church building. One day that week, I stepped from our transport vehicle to greet a group of twenty preschoolers—all of them fascinated by my hands. As they played with my fingers, through a translator I got to tell them about God's love.

Who am I, God, to have slept on the Rock of Gibraltar, walked the Roman Colosseum, and tented with my boys at the base of China's Great Wall? *Only God does things like this.*

On mission in the Dominican Republic (left), and in Africa (right)

In 2006, our family and another (close friends) moved to a city in East Asia on a two-year adventure in sport. There, we embraced a people and culture radically different, as God taught me to adapt, bringing further change to my life.

A twenty-eight-person passenger bus was to take us from the airport to a hotel where we'd planned to begin our stay. Off to a promising start, a local welcomed us to the country with a sign with our names on it. We snagged our twenty-three bags. Then eight of us—four adults with four kids (ages four to fourteen)—followed this stranger to the parking garage. He pointed to his car, a small minivan. Then his friend whipped around a corner, driving a mid-sized sedan. Fifteen minutes later, the two of them pressing the full weight of their bodies on our bags, it all fit—with our kids seated on our laps.

Episodes like this stretched and pressed me beyond my comfort zone.

Most mornings in Asia, I'd climb out of bed, find my Bible and step outside to an awning of our apartment on the nineteenth floor. It overlooked a small part of what was a huge, metropolitan city. I'd think: *I don't speak the language. Today I'll spend three hours in traffic. I might get three business meetings if I can figure out who I'm supposed to meet.* Often, I'd flip open God's Word to John, chapter 15 and a place I'd grooved to read: "Apart from Christ, I can do nothing" (John 15:5).

Situations were complicated and complex, and my plans were often frustrated. I felt I lacked control. When something went wrong, I lacked the competency to fix it. Unable to perform, limitations caused me to grow more humble—eventually learning more fully to trust God, by faith.

Over two decades, on a number of occasions I'd heard talks on "The Spirit-filled Life" (see Appendix B—*Satisfied?* on page 137). Until I lived overseas, I'd largely ignored this teaching to live and work in God-reliance, and experience His power.

Ephesians 5:17-18 exhorts me to live "filled with God's Holy Spirit." I'd known that God had provided His Holy Spirit to teach, guide, comfort and empower me to live my Christian life better. Through a discipline of "spiritual breathing," I've learned how to exhale the impure (confess any sins) and inhale the pure (His Spirit). Often, because of my want for control, I have to confess: "God, take me off the 'throne' (control center) of my life; fill me with Your Holy Spirit." It's a discipline I now do multiple times each day.

In 2008, we thought we'd leave East Asia to return to our home in Ohio. God, once more, had different plans. (I didn't see God's *whisper* coming.) We moved to Orlando, to the world headquarters of Cru.

At work with Cru/CCC president, Steve Douglass

In 2009, I received an unexpected invite to work closely with Cru's president and some of its global leaders. *With* God, I've had so many opportunities to help more people come to encounter Jesus in a relationship of love, forgiveness and grace—leading, coaching, strategizing, contributing and collaborating in the company of terrific and talented people. *Only God does this! I'm grateful.*

Uphill Climbs

Amidst these amazing opportunities, I've pedaled my share of uphill climbs. Every life has its difficulties.

A few years before the East Asia move, and at midlife (almost forty), I again met my foe—performance.

I'd stepped into an operations role, and, through unusual circumstances suddenly found myself the interim leader of a fairly broken team of twenty. The situation was new to me. I was in over my head, thinking I had to be the guy to fix it. Speedily, I acted and took steps devoid of good process. My inspiring pep talk made things worse. Within days, I knew I'd failed. (And I had.) So I buried myself

114

in what little I could control—budgets. Soon I'd become discouraged, and then weeks later, depressed. It was back to the counselor.

It took about three months, but God and the counselor convinced me that I'd never live on Earth free of faults. "No, Greg," he said. "Perfection happens when, in Jesus, you die and go to heaven. Then you'll see Him as He is; you'll be conformed to the likeness of Jesus." I thought: *What a day that will be.*

I can't explain it, but one day I rose to my feet on a dock where I'd fished, and I felt healed. God's grace felt sufficient for me. And I agreed with the counselor that I'd accept no more roles where I crunched numbers.

In our first week in Florida in 2008, our younger son Ryan nearly drowned in a swimming pool at our apartment complex. Ryan survived (praise God!) in spite of my negligence. Foolishly, I'd been reading a book even though Ryan was not yet able to swim. For a few weeks afterward, I felt ashamed, my heart heavy with guilt. *What was I thinking?* Then one morning (once more in a specific instant), I arose from a chair, feeling freed and forgiven. I'd known I'd been forgiven since hours after the incident when I'd confessed in prayer; however, I found it harder to forgive myself than others.

In fall 2011, our older son Kyle battled intense anxiety and then lapsed into depression. His junior year in high school was a difficult stretch. At times, Linda and I knew of nothing to do other than to turn to God in prayer. Within months, God led us to a resource we needed. With treatment, Kyle returned to health by his senior year. He graduated high school as valedictorian, now on his way to multiple degrees as a student and spiritual leader at the University of Florida. He regularly shares his story as a testimony of his faith.

In 2007, Coach Newberry died. In 2015, my stepfather Bob died, a war hero at the age of ninety-two. Today, my dad lives with dementia. We can't talk about sports and other things we loved to share as we once did.

Life is hard, yet God wastes nothing. Amidst all the enjoyable and good, God finds ways to whittle away my arrogance and pride. I'm glad, and I'm sure there's more to go. Obstacles remind me I'm human, and I don't have many of life's answers.

Always, and in everything, I need God. I give God praise in life's trials as well as in the successes I've enjoyed.

This life, in Jesus, is a truly amazing ride!

Rethink It

1. What "mountains" lie before you? How will you climb them? What will be your source of strength to do so?

2. If life is an adventure, how has a trial or negative circumstance (a limitation) positively impacted you?

3. Which is more difficult for you: to forgive another person or to forgive yourself? Why?

4. Write or share an experience that you count special—perhaps a moment of triumph in your life. Do you give God credit or praise for this? Think about and share in what ways God can use this experience for your good and perhaps for the good of others.

5. If you were to view life as a spiritual journey, how would you describe where you are?

6. What do you see as the relationship between faith and a person reaching his or her potential?

CHAPTER TEN

This Life—What a Ride

Your life is your message to the world. Make sure it is inspiring.

Unknown

A few years back, a three-day bicycle ride afforded me considerable time to reflect. Sitting astride a bicycle will do that.

On my ride through Iowa's cornfields, I gave thought to some highlights of my life and its major themes: 1) I've known unconditional love as a great gift—that of my parents, my wife, and my Creator, God, without whom there'd be no story. 2) Loved, I'm imperfectly human. I have a sin-nature that still fights for control. It nags me some days to do likewise in a quest for perfection that—this side of eternity in heaven—I have come to accept (most days) won't happen. 3) And point two is okay. Deeply beloved, a child of God, my true identity and worth now rests squarely in Jesus. In relationship with Jesus, I've rethought my life, unleashed my potential, and experienced life abundant on Earth with a promise of being with Him for eternity.

You've come this far; ride along with me if you will.

What a Ride

"Hey, Greg, I have a challenge for you." I recognized the voice of Darin, a friend I'd traveled with on a few basketball mission trips. Even though Darin was twenty years younger than I was, we'd become great friends.

"How about joining me on a bike ride through Iowa?" *Uh-oh, how long?* was my first thought. *Perhaps riding with a friend through rolling hills and passing fields of corn could provide a nice summer break.*

Indeed, what Darin had in mind struck me as a little more than a pleasure ride. He suggested I fly out to join him for part of the Des Moines Register's Annual Great Bike Ride Across Iowa—better known as the RAGBRAI. It's a seven-day trip across the state and about thirty-thousand people participate. This seemed a bicycle TREK!

He went on to explain: "My dad, Dave, will do the whole thing. My brother Dan and I are going to do about thirty to forty miles each day for three or four days. Why don't you come along?"

"Three days at thirty to forty miles? I can handle that," I replied. We'd enjoy one another's friendship while enjoying the heartland of America. "It sounds fun," I added. "I'm in."

Darin's call came in March. RAGBRAI took place in mid-July. Soon I'd found a good price on my airplane ticket and was excited about this new adventure—a bucket-list-like experience. *Do it once, I'm good.* Momentarily, I gave pause to how I'd not ceased to set goals as I did so much in my youth—glad, though, that my exhilaration from accolades and what I'd accomplished no longer defined me.

A week later, Darin sent me an email: "Dan and I have decided to do about sixty to seventy miles each day. What do you think?" It could be a stretch, but I responded, "With a little wind at my back, I can make it."

Two weeks later, another note appeared in my inbox: "Dan and I are going to do 110 miles the first day."

"Have fun doing that," I shot back. "You can drive back to get me!" Darin and Dan finally decided it wise to pedal fifty to seventy miles each of three consecutive days.

I hadn't ridden my bicycle much, but March in Florida is a fantastic time to do it. Occasionally, I'd cycled ten miles or so—once doing the nineteen miles in Colorado—but never more than that. I figured it was time to train.

I didn't mind the thought of putting in some work. I'd trained as a child, busying myself for hours trying to shape perfect golf shots or to toss free throws that swished the net. In school and projects at work, I'd disciplined myself to study and had reaped success. On a spiritual journey of growth, I'd matured in my faith through biblical training. Surely, I had it in me to prep my cycling muscles and pedal the miles required.

That was, until I got pneumonia in late May. Not until mid-June did I fully recover. It left me only four weeks to prepare. I had started with a plan; I had to work a different plan to train. I felt that if I could complete two fifty-mile rides in scorching Florida sun on a borrowed bike that didn't fit my legs or my rump, I could make it in Iowa.

A month later, my plane landed in Iowa. I rented a bicycle there, and the next morning straddled its seat.

Day One: Darin, Dan and I started a little outside Ames and pedaled northeast on our own fifty-four-mile county-road route. It was a sunny and pleasant seventy-five-degree day. Facing no problems, we enjoyed our time together, and I felt terrific.

Day Two: We were energized by meeting up with their dad, Dave, and the official RAGBRAI pack. By day's end, we had successfully ridden seventy miles with mild effort and more Iowa cornfields and small communities behind us. I'd had two days of personal-distance-bests.

Day Three: We awoke in Waverly, Iowa, to pouring rain. I grabbed a cup of coffee, threw on an oversized camouflage poncho, and hoisted myself up to the seat of my bike. Dan joined some friends of his that day, so Darin, a friend of his (John), his Dad and I rode in a pack.

Instantly we were drenched. Ferociously, I pumped my legs with a lean to the right, battling the thirty- to-forty-mph southerly gusts of wind. Temperatures had plummeted into the mid-fifties—cold for this Floridian. Locals described it as the worst day of weather in the event's thirty-year history—naturally, the only year I'd participate. It didn't take long for my muscles to tighten and scream.

My lips quivered, and my body shook. We'd survived twenty-eight miles when Dave suggested we break to warm ourselves in the lobby of some friend's office. That felt super—that is, until Dave flipped open the route map, pointed and said, "Greg, this is going to get tough." *Get tough? What's this been?* He added, "In two miles we're going to turn south, with a good part of the rest of today's ride into the wind."

I cranked my handlebars to the right and straight into the storm. Frigid droplets in a driving rain clouded my goggles and pummeled my body. I removed my goggles to the horrific sight of a three-mile-long hill—me on the wrong side of it. Thighs burning and legs finding it difficult to churn, I glanced at my odometer. It bounced between four and six mph, instead of the fifteen to seventeen mph we'd averaged. Ahead of me, Dave grew small. Darin was nowhere in sight. I'm no math whiz, as I've shared. Yet even I could compute my chafed butt on the seat for another eight hours at this pace. Mentally, and then physically, I felt I couldn't go much farther. I'd hit "the wall."

The wall is real. Runners "hit the wall" when, about nineteen miles into a 26.2-mile marathon, the mind and body decide they've had enough. It's time to quit. Negativity and doubt creep in as the desire to finish the race lapses.

I've hit the wall many times. As a youth, it happened with the chaos of our home. It happened with a move when a piece of my former identity, the sense that I belonged with a group of sports friends, was stripped away. Academically, I'd once wondered if I could graduate before slipping into advertising. In San Francisco, where my proclivity for alcohol spiraled out of control, I bottomed out. As a young adult, I'd hit that barrier of dating. And as a

Christian, perfectionism, or performance-based living, had taken its toll on occasion.

On my bicycle that day, my insides screamed "no mas," and I coasted to a stop on the shoulder. I felt done, for sure. Then, mercifully, Dave, a bit like a salmon swimming upstream, pedaled his way back toward me. Darin (and his friend John) soon pulled up beside. News to me: The two of them had collided when making the turn.

Dave, quick and spot-on in sizing up my despair, decided it time we change our approach. We needed a change of strategy. "We need a plan," Dave said. "I'll go first. John, you ride second and come to the front once in a while to give me a break. Darin, you ride third. Greg, you stay tight to Darin's back tire. Now, let's go." Riding close to one another's tires in a single-file line, we drafted up that hill.

Having watched NASCAR on TV, I'd seen drivers pull tight to one another's cars, saving gas or getting a literal pick-me-up from the speed of the car ahead of them to zoom past. Flocks of geese and other birds fly in V-formations to cut the wind by drafting.

In life, through the encouragement of others, I've often drafted. From my earliest days, I'd drafted in the acceptance, nurturing and coaching of my parents. Coach had coaxed me up that pegboard and inspired me to find a way to climb that rope seven times. On projects, with teammates or colleagues, I've drafted. Friends, mentors, pastors and counselors have provided valuable perspective. In them, I've also drafted.

Most of all, for almost thirty-five years now I've drafted daily, tucked tightly to God.

At my breaking point in September 1983, God intersected my life, drawing me to Jesus. My sins forgiven—my soul *made right* for eternity—I'd started a ride in which I'd hold tightly to Him.

Through the promises of God's Word, I draft. In those extended times alone, through His intimacy, guided by that whisper (a part of prayer), I draft. In relying on God's Spirit as opposed to my self-effort, I draft. When I work with God more than trying to work for Him, I focus less on performance and draft more closely to His will and His ways.

Drafting on the bicycle that day, I chugged up the hill with Dave, John and then Darin doing work for me. On one occasion I glanced behind me. A cyclist I didn't know had tucked himself tightly to my rear wheel. Behind him, a line of twenty riders in single-file scaled that Iowan hill.

I pedaled; it still wasn't easy. One time I broke formation and pumped frantically to pull even with Darin. "Hey," I shouted. "Your wife—she can drive in and get me at the next town, right? I think I'm done."

Darin shot me a look and said a few words—*just enough* for me to zip my lip, fall back and keep tackling the hill at double-speed, a pace of eight to ten mph.

An hour later, we turned left, to the east. After having beaten the headwind, the cross-breeze was of no consequence. The rain stopped. The sun peeked through the clouds. We coasted into the next farm community and, hungry for lunch, we found a restaurant with a buffet. There we grazed for ninety minutes on guilt-free calories to replace the ones we'd burned.

Twenty miles later we got to Independence, Iowa—a place where I'd envisioned freedom from our bikes. We'd ridden our 68.5 miles, and I felt exhausted—and yet for some reason I didn't feel done. "Good job, Darin," I said, "but we can't quit yet." He gave me an inquisitive look. "If we ride another 2.5 miles, we'll both have new personal bests."

Slowly, we joy-rode a few city streets and watched for the odometer to reach seventy-one miles—*just enough*. We tossed our bicycles to the ground and limped our way to Dairy Queen for behemoth ice-cream Blizzards to celebrate having finished.

One-hundred and ninety-five miles in three days. We'd made it! I felt fulfilled to have finished.

The Rest of the Story

Do you recall that moment in Iowa, and the time I broke formation and pedaled alongside Darin to suggest that I quit—that his wife come pick me up? With wisdom beyond his years, Darin told me just what I needed to hear: "Greg, you can't quit now. If you quit now, there is no story!"

It's been an amazing five decades. And Lord willing, it's hardly time to quit.

I have more days on Earth to live. More wonderful experiences, more times of challenge, more mess-ups, more opportunities to become a bit "more right" in this life—more like my Savior, Jesus.

Then there's the rest of the story. The best is yet to come.

God's Word says that in heaven, I'll be like Jesus, fully conformed to His image: perfected in His likeness, with a heart of no sin and even a physical body made complete. Ten fingers and ten toes: *Thanks, God. I'm not sure I'll need them, but I'll accept them as Your gift. I'm more excited about the rest of the package—a heart and mind renewed.*

I'll keep pedaling. I'm NOT perfected; here on Earth I won't be. But I'm on my way!

Some days here remain hard. Life has its pains. I don't know what tomorrow holds, yet I know He holds my tomorrows. Keep riding. *Keep pedaling. The best is yet to come!*

"So we're not giving up. How could we! Even though on the outside it looks like things are falling apart on us, on the inside, where God is making new life, not a day goes by without His unfolding grace. These hard times are small potatoes compared to the coming good times, the lavish celebration prepared for us. There's far more here than meets the eye. [You can believe it!] The things we see now are here today, gone tomorrow. But the things we can't see now will last forever" (2 Corinthians 4:16-18, The Message).

What a ride! What a ride, indeed!

Rethink It

1. In what areas of your life do you feel like you've "hit the wall"?

2. Could you pursue any training that would be of help?

3. Are there friends or others you know who could help you to "draft" beyond what presently limits you?

4. How can you be available and encourage others to draft behind you?

5. How better could you draft in relationship to God?

6. At life's end, what would you most want family, friends, and others to remember?

7. How can you believe, think and feel differently in order to unleash your potential and finish your life well?

APPENDIX A

Would You Like to Know God Personally?

This booklet contains a message of love and hope. An exciting adventure awaits all who discover these life-changing truths. The following four principles will help you discover how to know God personally and experience the abundant life He promised.

God's Perspective	God loves you and created you to know Him personally. He has a wonderful plan for your life.

God's Love

"For God so loved the world that He gave His one and only Son, that whoever believes in Him shall not perish but have eternal life" (John 3:16, NIV).

God's Plan

"Now this is eternal life: that they may know you, the only true God, and Jesus Christ, whom you have sent" (John 17:3).

▶ *What prevents us from knowing God personally?*

Our Condition	People are sinful and separated from God, so we cannot know Him personally or experience His love and plan.

People are Sinful

"...for all have sinned and fall short of the glory of God" (Romans 3:23).

People were created to have fellowship with God; but, because of our stubborn self-will, we chose to go our own independent way and fellowship with God was broken. This self-will, characterized by an attitude of active rebellion or passive indifference, is evidence of what the Bible calls sin.

People are Separated

"For the wages of sin is death" [spiritual separation from God] (Romans 6:23).

This diagram illustrates that God is holy and people are sinful. A great gulf separates the two. The arrows illustrate that people are continually trying to reach God and establish a personal relationship with Him through our own efforts, such as a good life, philosophy, or religion, but we inevitably fail.

▶ *The third principle explains the only way to bridge this gulf...*

God's Response

Jesus Christ is God's only provision for our sin. through Him alone we can know God personally an experience God's love and plan.

He Died in Our Place

"But God demonstrates His own love for us in this: While we were still sinners, Christ died for us" (Romans 5:8).

He Rose From the Dead

"...Christ died for our sins ... He was buried, He was raised on the third day according to the Scriptures ... He appeared to Peter, and then to the Twelve. After that, He appeared to more than five hundred ..." (1 Corinthians 15:3–6).

He is the Only Way to God

"Jesus answered, 'I am the way and the truth and the life. No one comes to the Father except through Me'" (John 14:6).

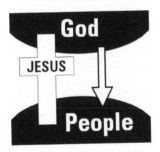

This diagram illustrates that God has bridged the gulf that separates us from Him by sending His Son, Jesus Christ, to die on the cross in our place to pay the penalty for our sins.

It is not enough to know these truths.

▶ *What prevents us from knowing God personally?*

Our Response

We must individually receive Jesus Christ as Savior and Lord; then we can know God personally and experience His love and plan.

We Must Receive Christ

"Yet to all who received Him, to those who believed in His name, He gave the right to become children of God" (John 1:12).

We Receive Christ Through Faith

"For it is by grace you have been saved, through faith—and this not from yourselves, it is the gift of God—not by works, so that no one can boast" (Ephesians 2:8,9).

When We Receive Christ, We Experience a New Birth (Read John 3:1–8).

We Receive Christ by Personal Invitation

[Christ speaking] *"Here I am! I stand at the door and knock. If anyone hears My voice and opens the door, I will come in and eat with him, and he with Me" (Revelation 3:20).*

Receiving Christ involves turning to God from self (repentance) and trusting Christ to come into our lives to forgive us of our sins and to make us what He wants us to be. Just to agree intellectually that Jesus Christ is the Son of God and that He died on the cross for our sins is not enough. Nor is it enough to have an emotional experience. We receive Jesus Christ by faith, as an act of the will.

These two circles represent two kinds of lives.

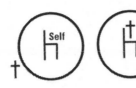

A life without Jesus Christ.
Self is in the center and on the throne; Christ (†) is outside.

A life entrusted to Christ.
Christ is in the center and on the throne, and Self yields to Christ.

Which circle best describes your life?
Which circle would you like to have represent your life?

▶ *The following explains how you can receive Christ...*

You Can Receive Christ Right Now by Faith Through Prayer

(Prayer is talking with God.)

God knows your heart and is not as concerned with your words as He is with the attitude of your heart. The following is a suggested prayer:

Lord Jesus, I want to know You personally. Thank You for dying on the cross for my sins. I open the door of my life and receive You as my Savior and Lord. Thank You for forgiving me of my sins and giving me eternal life. Take control of the throne of my life. Make me the kind of person You want me to be.

Does this prayer express the desire of your heart?

If it does, pray this prayer right now, and Christ will come into your life, as He promised.

How to Know That Christ is in Your Life

Did you receive Christ into your life?

According to His promise as recorded in Revelation 3:20, where is Christ right now in relation to you? Christ said that He would come into your life and be your Savior and friend so you can know Him personally. Would He mislead you? On what authority do you know that God has answered your prayer? (The trustworthiness of God Himself and His Word.)

The Bible Promises Eternal Life to All Who Receive Christ

"And this is the testimony: God has given us eternal life, and this life is in His Son. He who has the Son has life; he who does not have the Son of God does not have life. I write these things to you who believe in the name of the Son of God so that you may know that you have eternal life" (1 John 5:11–13).

Thank God often that Christ is in your life and that He will never leave you (Hebrews 13:5). You can know on the basis of His promise that Christ lives in you and that you have eternal life from the very moment you invite Him in.

▶ *An important reminder...*

Do Not Depend on Feelings

The promise of God's Word, the Bible—not our feelings—is our authority. The Christian lives by faith (trust) in the trustworthiness of

God Himself and His Word. Flying in a jet can illustrate the relationship among fact (God and His Word), faith (our trust in God and His Word), and feeling (the result of our faith and obedience) (see John 14:21).

To be transported by a jet, we must place our faith in the

trustworthiness of the aircraft and the pilot who flies it. Our feelings of confidence or fear do not affect the ability of the jet to transport us, though they do affect how much we enjoy the trip. In the same way, we as Christians do not depend on feelings or emotions, but we place our faith (trust) in the trustworthiness of God and the promises of His Word.

Now That You Have Entered Into a Personal Relationship With Christ

The moment you received Christ by faith, as an act of your will, many things happened, including the following:

- Christ came into your life (Revelation 3:20 and Colossians 1:27).
- Your sins were forgiven (Colossians 1:14).
- You became a child of God (John 1:12).
- You received eternal life (John 5:24).
- You began the great adventure for which God created you (John 10:10; 2 Corinthians 5:17 and 1 Thessalonians 5:18).

Can you think of anything more wonderful that could happen to you than entering into a personal relationship with Jesus Christ? Would you like to thank God in prayer right now for what He has done for you? By thanking God, you demonstrate your faith.

▶ *To enjoy your new relationship with God...*

135

Suggestions For Christian Growth

Spiritual growth results from trusting Jesus Christ. "…The righteous will live by faith" (Galatians 3:11). A life of faith will enable you to trust God increasingly with every detail of your life, and to practice the following:

G   Go to God in prayer daily (John 15:7).
R   Read God's Word daily (Acts 17:11). Begin with the Gospel of John.
O   Obey God moment by moment (John 14:21).
W   Witness for Christ by your life and words (Matthew 4:19; John 15:8).
T   Trust God for every detail of your life (1 Peter 5:7).
H   Holy Spirit—Allow Him to control and empower your daily life and witness (Galatians 5:16,17; Acts 1:8).

Remember

Your walk with Christ depends on what you allow Him to do in and through you empowered by the Holy Spirit, not what you do for Him through self effort.

Fellowship in a Good Church

God's Word admonishes us, "Let us not give up meeting together…" (Hebrews 10:25). Several logs burn brightly together; but put one aside on the cold hearth and the fire goes out. So it is with your relationship with other Christians. If you do not belong to a church, do not wait to be invited. Take the initiative; call the pastor of a nearby church where Christ is honored and His Word is preached. Start this week, and make plans to attend regularly.

If you still have questions, visit: www.whoisJesus-really.com or www.everystudent.com

APPENDIX B

Satisfied?

Satisfaction: (n.) fulfillment of one's needs, longings, or desires

What words would you use to describe your current experience as a Christian?

Growing	Empty	Frustrated	Discouraged
Disappointing	Duty	Fulfilled	Intimate
Forgiven	Mediocre	Stuck	Painful
Struggling	Dynamic	Joyful	Guilty
Defeated	Vital	Exciting	So-so
Up and down	...*Others?*		

Do you desire more? Jesus said, *"If anyone is thirsty, let him come to me and drink. Whoever believes in me, as the Scripture has said, streams of living water will flow from within him" (John 7:37, 38).*

What did Jesus mean? John, the biblical author, went on to explain, *"By this he meant the Spirit, whom those who believed in him were later to receive. Up to that time the Spirit had not been given, since Jesus had not yet been glorified" (John 7:39).*

Jesus promised that God's Holy Spirit would satisfy the thirst, or deepest longings, of all who believe in Jesus Christ. However, many Christians do not understand the Holy Spirit or how to experience Him in their daily lives.

▶ *The following principles will help you understand and enjoy God's Spirit.*

The Divine Gift	God has given us His Spirit so that we can experience intimacy with Him and enjoy all He has for us.

The Holy Spirit is the source of our deepest satisfaction.

The Holy Spirit is God's permanent presence with us.

Jesus said, *"And I will ask the Father, and he will give you another Counselor to be with you forever—the Spirit of truth"* *(John 14:16, 17).*

The Holy Spirit enables us to understand and experience all God has given us.

"We have not received the spirit of the world but the Spirit who is from God, that we may understand what God has freely given us" (1 Corinthians 2:12).

The Holy Spirit enables us to experience many things:
- **A genuine new spiritual life** (John 3:1–8).
- **The assurance of being a child of God** (Romans 8:15, 16).
- **The infinite love of God** (Romans 5:5; Ephesians 3:18, 19).

Life Without the Spirit	Life With the Spirit
Before Receiving Christ	After Receiving Christ

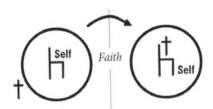

The man without the Spirit does not accept the things that come from the Spirit of God, for they are foolishness to him, and he cannot understand them, because they are spiritually discerned. (1 Corinthians 2:14).	The spiritual man makes judgments about all things…We have the mind of Christ (1 Cor. 2:15, 16). But those who are controlled by the Holy Spirit think about things that please the Spirit (Romans 8:5, NLT).

▶ *Why are many Christians not satisfied in their experience with God?*

The Present Danger

Danger: (n.) a thing that may cause injury, loss, or pain

We cannot experience intimacy with God and enjoy all He has for us if we fail to depend on His Spirit.

People who trust in their own efforts and strength to live the Christian life will experience failure and frustration, as will those who live to please themselves rather than God.

We cannot live the Christian life in our own strength.

> *"Are you so foolish? After beginning with the Spirit, are you now trying to attain your goal by human effort?"* *(Galatians 3:3).*

We cannot enjoy all God desires for us if we live by our self-centered desires.

> *"For the sinful nature desires what is contrary to the Spirit, and the Spirit what is contrary to the sinful nature. They are in conflict with each other, so that you do not do what you want"* *(Galatians 5:17).*

Three Kinds of Lifestyles

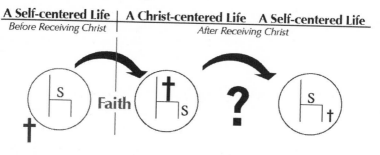

Read 1 Corinthians 3:1-3 on the next page.

"Brothers, I could not address you as spiritual, but as worldly—mere infants in Christ. I gave you milk, not solid food, for you were not yet ready for it. Indeed, you are still not ready. You are still worldly. For since there is jealousy and quarreling among you, are you not worldly? Are you not acting like mere men?"
(1 Corinthians 3:1–3).

▶ **How can we develop a lifestyle of depending on the Spirit?**

The Intimate Journey

By walking in the Spirit we increasingly experience intimacy with God and enjoy all He has for us.

Journey: (n.) any course from one experience to another

Walking in the Spirit moment by moment is a lifestyle. It is learning to depend upon the Holy Spirit for His abundant resources as a way of life.

As we walk in the Spirit, we have the ability to live a life pleasing to God.

"So I say, live by the Spirit, and you will not gratify the desires of the sinful nature...Since we live by the Spirit, let us keep in step with the Spirit" (Galatians 5:16, 25).

As we walk in the Spirit, we experience intimacy with God and all He has for us.

"But the fruit of the Spirit is love, joy, peace, patience, kindness, goodness, faithfulness, gentleness, and self-control" (Galatians 5:22, 23).

The Christ-centered Life

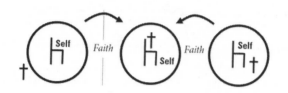

Faith (trust in God and His promises) is the only way a Christian can live by the Spirit.

Spiritual breathing is a powerful word picture which can help you experience moment-by-moment dependence upon the Spirit.

Exhale: Confess your sin the moment you become aware of it—agree with God concerning it and thank Him for His forgiveness, according to 1 John 1:9 and Hebrews 10:1–25. Confession requires repentance—a change in attitude and action.

Inhale: Surrender control of your life to Christ, and rely upon the Holy Spirit to fill you with His presence and power by faith, according to His **command** (Ephesians 5:18) and **promise** (1 John 5:14, 15).

▶ *How does the Holy Spirit fill us with His power?*

The Empowering Presence

We are filled with the Spirit by faith, enabling us to experience intimacy with God and enjoy all He has for us.

Empower: (v.) to give ability to

The essence of the Christian life is what God does in and through us, not what we do for God. Christ's life is reproduced in the believer by the power of the Holy Spirit. To be filled with the Spirit is to be directed and empowered by Him.

By faith, we experience God's power through the Holy Spirit.

> *"I pray that out of his glorious riches he may strengthen you with power through his Spirit in your inner being, so that Christ may dwell in your hearts through faith" (Ephesians 3:16, 17).*

Three important questions to ask yourself:

1. Am I ready now to surrender control of my life to our Lord Jesus Christ? (Romans 12:1, 2)
2. Am I ready now to confess my sins? (1 John 1:9) Sin grieves God's Spirit (Ephesians 4:30). But God in His love has forgiven all of your sins—past, present, and future—because Christ has died for you.
3. Do I sincerely desire to be directed and empowered by the Holy Spirit? (John 7:37–39)

By faith claim the fullness of the Spirit according to His command and promise:

God **COMMANDS** us to be filled with the Spirit.

"...be filled with the Spirit" (Ephesians 5:18).

God **PROMISES** He will always answer when we pray according to His will.

> *"This is the confidence we have in approaching God: that if we ask anything according to his will, he hears us. And if we know that he hears us—whatever we ask—we know that we have what we asked of him" (1 John 5:14, 15).*

▶ *How to pray to be filled with the Holy Spirit...*

The Turning Point

Turning point: time when a decisive change occurs

We are filled with the Spirit by faith alone.

Sincere prayer is one way of expressing our faith. The following is a suggested prayer:

Dear Father, I need You. I acknowledge that I have sinned against You by directing my own life. I thank You that You have forgiven my sins through Christ's death on the cross for me. I now invite Christ to again take His place on the throne of my life. Fill me with the Holy Spirit as You commanded me to be filled, and as You promised in Your Word that You would do if I asked in faith. I pray this in the name of Jesus. I now thank You for filling me with the Holy Spirit and directing my life.

Does this prayer express the desire of your heart? If so, you can pray right now and trust God to fill you with His Holy Spirit.

How to know that you are filled by the Holy Spirit

- Did you ask God to fill you with the Holy Spirit?
- Do you know that you are now filled with the Holy Spirit?
- On what authority? (On the trustworthiness of God Himself and His Word: Hebrews 11:6; Romans 14:22, 23.)

As you continue to depend on God's Spirit moment by moment you will experience and enjoy intimacy with God and all He has for you—a truly rich and satisfying life.

An important reminder ...

Do Not Depend on Feelings

The promise of God's Word, the Bible—not our feelings—is our authority. The Christian lives by faith (trust) in the trustworthiness of God Himself and His Word. Flying in an airplane can illustrate the relationship among fact (*God and His Word*), faith (*our trust in God and His Word*), and feeling (*the result of our faith and obedience*) (John 14:21).

To be transported by an airplane, we must place our faith in the trustworthiness of the aircraft and the pilot who flies it. Our feelings of confidence or fear do not affect the ability of the airplane to transport us, though they do affect how much we enjoy the trip. In the same way, we as Christians do not depend on feelings or emotions, but we place our faith (trust) in the trustworthiness of God and the promises of His Word.

Now That You are Filled with the Holy Spirit

Thank God that the Spirit will enable you:

- To glorify Christ with your life (John 16:14).
- To grow in your understanding of God and His Word (1 Corinthians 2:14, 15).
- To live a life pleasing to God (Galatians 5:16–23).

Remember the promise of Jesus:

"But you will receive power when the Holy Spirit comes on you; and you will be my witnesses in Jerusalem, and in all Judea and Samaria, and to the ends of the earth" (Acts 1:8).

Are you a fan of this book?

Here are some practical ways you can help me share this message with others.

- Share it with friends and family.
- Post about the book on your social media; added copies available on Amazon.com.
- Write a positive review about the book on Amazon.com.
- Next time you are in a bookstore ask if they carry a copy. If not, ask them to order one for you.
- Mention the book at clubs, churches, and organizations you attend.
- Consider using it as part of a small group you lead.
- Contact me about special bulk quantity discounts.
- Help further the distribution of this book with a donation to the ministry of Greg and Linda Stoughton with Cru give.cru.org/0359850.

I'd love to hear about specific changes you're making as a result of reading this book.

- You can personally email me about your life-change at greg@gregstoughton.com.

Book me to speak at your next event.

- Send an email with details about your event at greg@gregstoughton.com.

Order more copies of this book on Amazon.com.

ABOUT THE AUTHOR

Greg is a leader, strategic thinker, mentor and speaker with a passion to help others embrace their full potential as they discover God's purpose and plan for their lives. He daily seeks to add value to the lives of others.

He and his wife Linda both serve on staff with Cru (formerly Campus Crusade for Christ). Greg has served at Cru for more than 25 years in a wide range of leadership roles, including Director of Communications and Director of Basketball Operations for Athletes in Action. Greg currently serves as Associate Chief of Staff for the President of Cru.

In 2001, in West Chester, Ohio, he launched with a few friends what is now the nation's largest chapter of Upward Basketball—1500 children each year involved in a collaborative effort of ten churches. In 1996, Greg authored with Coach Joe Gibbs: "Fourth and One: A Bible Study for Men."

He graduated from the University of Oregon, Eugene, in 1983 (B.S., Journalism/Advertising). He received his Masters of Theological Studies in 2011 from Bakke Graduate University, Seattle.

Greg has two sons and resides in the Central Florida area. A few of Greg's hobbies include: spectating sports, golf, travel and kayak fishing with his younger son.

For more information, or to request Greg to speak, contact him at greg@gregstoughton.com.

Made in the USA
San Bernardino, CA
04 July 2017